My Grace to You

Written By:

mike hillebrecht

My Grace to You

ISBN-13 978-0615686622

ISBN-10 0615686621

Scripture quotations are from the King James Version.

Other Books by mike hillebrecht

Grace for Shame

Chesed – Beyond the Veil of Mercy

Your Life is a Freaking Mess and You Want Answers

A Kingdom Primer

Eternal Life. Yes, Forever!

Published by

Charis Academy Publishing

Portland, Oregon

www.charisacademy.org

ENDORSEMENTS

This book, *"My Grace to You"* is a must read for anyone that is serious about their walk with God. As an Ambassador of a nation, and my extensive travels around the world, I have not found a more important book to aid the Kingdom of God then this one. Mike please keep writing - the world needs you.

Ambassador Clyde Rivers, Republic of Burundi

Contents

Preface

This book is the fifth in a series of books I've written about the Kingdom of God, which is fitting if you find any significance in the meaning of numbers. The biblical meaning of the number five is grace. I assure you that I did not purposely delay this manuscript to make this point evident. My first book, *Grace for Shame, The Kingdom Solution to Reigning* contains some of the material which was revealed to me about the nature of grace and its importance in overcoming the shame that plagues so many believers even years after being saved.

There is however a wealth of understanding which eludes believers about a very important aspect of their new nature. Foremost, I believe, is a relevant discovery of the operation of grace. Not the grace so many have grown up with handed down from the traditions of many tear-stained grandmothers of the faith. What I mean is the grace Jesus and the apostles operated from.

In these writings I will incorporate some of the material from *Grace for Shame* and my other books in order to give you a foundation; however, I will expand beyond it so you can better see the vastness of what grace represents in our lives.

Warning: This material is written from the perspective of the Kingdom of God, not from the fall of man. This is vital in how you use this material. Most of the teachings we've had about grace have been focused from the position of the fall of man. This skews the understanding and implementation of grace considerably since it makes grace an escape mechanism rather than a tool of empowerment as it was originally intended.

Having said that, I want to clear up one thing right from the start: I am not writing a religious message. I say this because grace has been used by organizational moral leaders (i.e., religion) throughout history as a tool to capture those with a world view who were opposed to their message. While many of their intentions may have been worthy, often the actions they took produced a result completely opposite to the message delivered. The original definition of the term "religion," as it comes from the Latin word *religare*, means "to bind or tie up again." Jesus, who is the representation of grace from the Kingdom of God, came to set the captives free. Therefore, this message is focused towards freedom, not the practice of religion.

You are about to venture into a world which is not like anything you have ever experienced. I can boldly proclaim this about the Kingdom of God because today many just don't understand how the Kingdom operates, even though it was the only message Jesus preached about. Unfortunately, there is a slight dilemma to what you are about to read here that I'm willing to recognize right up front: You think you know what I'm going to talk about, so you'll probably only skim through this and see if there is anything "new" you don't know. Let me explain.

In the book *The 21 Irrefutable Laws of Leadership* by John Maxwell, he states one of the laws in leadership is known as the "Law of the Lid." Simply put, this law suggests that every organization will only rise to the level of the person which leads it. If the leader is rated as a seven, the organization can only rise to the level of a six because the leader is the lid at the position of seven. This law even applies in a church environment! Have you ever been frustrated when the pastor doesn't ever get to the "meat" of the matter in a service? He is dealing with the lid, but it's not one that he controls. This lid is what I call the "Mrs. Jones Effect."

Our brains are wonderfully and marvelously made to take in a variety of information through numerous receptors in our bodies. As we process this information, we begin to recognize patterns in events and begin creating catalogues of these patterns as a way of being able to efficiently work with all the information. Some of these catalogues of patterns become our beliefs, and over time, they have become so ingrained that when we even begin to see the first occurrence of a pattern, we instantly acknowledge it resembles a particular catalogue and subsequently activates our "long-held" belief. Put another way, our present perceptions are built from past events. So why do I call this the "Mrs. Jones Effect?"

If you were raised in a church environment from a child, you probably had a Mrs. Jones in the child ministry. Her ministry gift was her ability to keep a class of small children quiet and occupied during the 45 minutes that the adult service lasted. Any spiritual lessons provided were designed to be simple in context so they could be accomplished in the time frame dictated by the length of the grown-up message. These lessons (i.e., The Fall of Man, Noah and the Flood, Samson, David and Goliath, Jesus Walks on the Water, and of course the Christmas/Easter stories) were repeated frequently during the child's formative years. From these lessons, we developed our spiritual catalogue of beliefs. Regrettably, these lessons have become your lid!

Now I understand that some of you may never have been raised in this type of environment. You came to Christ as an adult, so "The Mrs. Jones Effect" can't apply to you, right? Consider this: Is the person instructing you in your congregation a past student of Mrs. Jones?[1]

This is the lid which your pastor has to deal with weekly. Some beliefs are just plain stuck in Mrs. Jones' class, and he can only present certain truths a little at a time, since it is so difficult to pull the lid off of what Mrs. Jones has created.

So I trust that you now realize my dilemma in presenting this material to you. You have a belief in what the topic is about. This belief is not right or wrong; it is your belief, or a perception based on pasted events. My question to you is this: Are you willing to take the lid off of your belief and question why you believe what you believe? Are you willing to look at your belief in a whole new manner which can make you more empowered? The main way to change any perception is to ask questions. In this material I'll be asking a lot of questions.

It will be my purpose on the following pages to convey an aspect of grace to you which will enable you to break free from the shackles which have held you back from fulfilling the destiny which God has created you to have. Some of this material will come directly from the book's website, www.mygrace2u.com while other parts will be fresh from the oven, so to speak. It is not my intent to regurgitate someone else's teaching material here but to show you what has been shown to me and, if need be, use other material as a springboard to advance further into the revelation.

Those who know me, call me, "Teacher." This, I believe, is the grace-gift given long before I was "saved." You will find employed in the following pages techniques which can only come from one who enjoys teaching others. I enjoy knowing what a word truly means in all of its various forms, but I don't like to be bogged down in the

---

[1] Mrs. Jones is a fictional character that I have created to demonstrate a point. If your name is Mrs. Jones and you work in child ministry, I have the greatest respect for you and your gift. I trust that you will be able to recognize my point in this matter and understand that the lessons that you present to our children are a vital component to developing a strong spiritual character.

"intellectual pursuit" of knowing just to know. I also want to understand why someone says something the way they do, so historical matters and social customs help me to comprehend this. These two tools are the underpinning of the "how and why" I write the way I do.

Additionally, you will possibly arrive at a point in reading this material when you suddenly realize that I may have already said previously what you're presently reading. This is intentional. One of the tools a teacher often employs is repetition in presenting material. When you look at the facets of a diamond, what are you truly looking at? You're looking into the center of the gem. Every facet opens a window into the exact same spot. The facets of grace covered in this book will all lead you into the same place in the Kingdom, so pay attention to what is repeated because it's a point worth remembering.

Someone once said every truly great writer writes for an audience of one: themselves. So in these pages which I write for myself, I trust you will gain the insight to help make your life all God intended it to be.

Hebrews 4:12 tells us God's word is living today just as it was when it was spoken and written down so many years ago. For those of you, who get hung up on the tense used in a manuscript, relax. If something is still living, its presence is present today. This was the choice I made throughout this work. It's not about what God did; it's about what He is doing still with the same words.

You can't write a book about grace without giving thanks to those who made it possible. To my wife, Kari; my great friends, Dr. Barry and Dr. Shawn; to Judy, Kim, Joyce, Dr. Richard, Craig, Linda, Sharon, Paul and all my immediate and extended family, I extend my *charis* to you. Also, to the one who made all of this possible, my Father, my Brother, and my Comforter. Thanks, for the grace from you.

A Starting Place

"Grace. It is important. Study!"

This is what I heard, not as a voice coming from around me, since my wife and I were in a meeting with over 1000 people listening to the same speaker. No, this voice came up out of the inside of me. Clear, and very authoritative. I did not question this familiar voice because I knew that it was Holy Spirit giving me my next assignment.

Whenever I speak about grace the inevitable question arises as to how I became so consumed with studying the subject. My wife and I were attending a conference in Redding, California (yes, we were at that church!) and it was the last night. The speaker was about to teach us on the power of our decree. I had no idea I was about to be invited into an environment which would forever change my life and its purpose. So what was the invitation? It came in the form of this verse:

> Let no corrupt speech proceed out of your mouth, but such as is good for edifying as the need may be, that it may give **grace** to them that hear. (Ephesians 4:29)

When we read that passage, instantly is when I heard Holy Spirit speak those words, *"Grace. It is important. Study!"* From that moment on, I did not hear one more word which was spoken. I had been commissioned. My gifting is to teach, and when you're commanded to study, it's like turning a pit bull loose on an 8-year old bully in a fenced yard. (All right, maybe not the most pleasant thought but it clearly gets the point across.) I had been spending the prior four months studying the scriptures on the various differences of time, specifically the Greek terms *chronos* and *kairos*, what their differences were, and where they occurred. This passage built upon what I had just learned and now poured into me a realm which, at that moment, I had no point of reference for. All I knew was that I was "saved by grace" and that was it.

I have learned a few things about this matter of grace since then, so let me provide you with an amplified rendition of this verse as I have come to personally understand it.

> *Let no rotten, time-based, foul or abusive words proceed out of your mouth but that which is intrinsically good and beneficial, suitable, as adorning a building with a new addition, properly designed with respect to the occupant's purpose and mission, in order that it may impart from the wealth of the abundance that you possess the joyously reciprocal gift of grace, thereby being and receiving encouragement to those that hear them. (Ephesians 4:29 amplified by mike)*

So how many of you got this same translation from the first example when you read it? Here is the bigger question: How many of you are fully realizing this amplified version in your communication? (For your information, I'm still working towards this end too. But I am closer today.) Contained within this one scripture, as with many more which I'm about to show you, there lies a treasure trove from the Kingdom of God. So I'm going to take you through a walk in my field of immeasurable price and show you what I've uncovered. This will take a little exploring, but at least you'll know what the terrain looks like when I'm done.

CLEARING THE DEBRIS

I like to know where you are before heading into new territory - it's a "teacher" thing. Here is what I want you to do. Take a moment to collect your thoughts and then create an imaginary red wagon. Next, I want you to take hold of every thought and word that is, or represents what grace means to you and put it into the wagon. Stack it as high as you need too. What is important is getting everything in there.

Make sure you get the word grace in there. However, don't forget gracious, grateful, gratitude, grace period, grace note, and of course don't forget gratuity. But while you're at it throw in charity, thankful, merciful, compassionate, pleasing, hospitable, cordial, charitable, stately, and social. Sometimes the best way to define something is to describe what it's not. So throw ungrateful, thankless, inhospitable, unmerciful, heartless, unsociable and inconsiderate into the wagon too.

You're not done though. What are the representations you have of grace? Did you include the way a dancer glides across the floor, or maybe how your favorite athlete performs under pressure? What about the way that a host or hostess at a dinner party conducts themselves? Did you consider the manner in which a horse runs on the range? What about the waiter or waitress who is able to carry both arms full of orders through a crowded restaurant? How about the spectacle of a sailboat cutting through the water on a sunny day? Obviously, there are more which I haven't touched on that you have labeled as grace. So put them in the wagon.

Now that you've got your red wagon filled with grace, I want you to go and park it somewhere in the corner of the room and don't go near it until you've finished reading this book. I know this act may be difficult, especially if you're a slow reader, however, we can't have what you think you know about grace influence the content. Don't worry, you'll get all of those words and thoughts back. You will find them to be a richer treasure when this process is done. Some of them you may not even want to retain, but this will be something for you to decide - later!

Let's Start

All right, so you claim, just like I did, that you're a sinner saved by grace. So what? I'll tell you right up front, today, I'm not the least bit impressed. Apparently, you have bought into some program dating back to the turn of the last century and don't understand what you're claiming. I know, because I bought into the same program and even have the cassette tapes (yes, cassette tapes!) to prove it. However, the truth that the Kingdom of God has already claimed about who you truly are is missing in your profession.

Harsh, I realize, but someone needs to snap you out of the stupor you're living in. Remember, you are no longer sitting under the influence of Mrs. Jones' class.[2] From this moment forward, you will no longer be permitted to use the words "sinner" and "grace" in the same sentence. This is the Kingdom of God, and in case you haven't realized it yet, He has taken care of the sin issue almost two thousand years ago. You now live from, and in, the grace of His kingdom.

Jesus did not come on Earth to bring another religion; He came to bring an everlasting government. This government operates from a throne and the results of its edicts are called "grace." The vast majority of believers do not understand how this government operates, what their place is within it, or even how to obtain the benefits due them. Let's look at what God's word states about this Kingdom reality in your life:

---

[2] If you're puzzled by that statement then you obviously have skipped over the forward of the book where I covered this.

Let us therefore come boldly unto the throne of grace, that we may obtain mercy, and find grace to help in time of need. (Hebrews 4:16)

This verse, not withstanding the opening verse of this chapter, will ultimately be what I'm working you towards. It holds so much power to us as believers, yet if you misunderstand just one word, all of its power is lost. Regrettably, there is the potential to misunderstand at least six words in this one verse! I'm not only talking about knowing the meaning of a word but the context in which the word is being used. Consider from this verse these words/terms: 1.) Boldly; 2.) throne; 3.) grace; 4.) mercy; 5.) time; 6.) need. Lastly, consider just who this verse, and book, was written to.

I know when most people look at a numerical list like this they think that I'm going to address each of these items one by one. Sorry. I'm not inclined to follow your conditioning. My purpose is to give you an understanding of grace, which will move you into this verse. If I was to focus all my attention on this one verse, many might be prone to latch onto what I uncover and create a doctrine from it. Yet we all know you can't make a doctrine from one verse, right?

So why use this verse as a starting place? It contains all the elements of the Kingdom of God that this study will be conducted from. This is, in my opinion, possibly the grandest picture of the Kingdom's daily operation in the lives of believers recorded in all the epistles. So my purpose is to get you to see what I see in this verse and in the process, permit you to explore new areas too.

GRACE IS A VERB... SO ACT THAT WAY!

It is amazing how God will readjust your perceptions about a topic when you least expect it (like the opening to this chapter!) I was reading recently a newsletter I receive from Michael Michalko who is known worldwide as an expert in creative thinking. Michael made the following comment:

Few of us understand that creativity is not a noun. It is a verb. Verbs are thinking, creating, sculpting, painting, making, dancing, singing, acting, searching, seizing, preparing, growing, reaping, seeing, knowing. Now when you take a verb that is alive and vibrant and turn it into a dead noun or principle that reeks of rules: something living dies.

This statement jarred me! The Holy Spirit then said to me, *"Grace is a verb."*

Noun or Verb Tense

In school each of us is taught the proper designation for words as they appear in their many representations. Nouns, we were told, are a person, place or thing, while verbs are action words. We also are instructed in the use of modifiers like pronouns, adjectives and adverbs which further describe the noun or verb it is associated with. Much of the church modifies their salvation from a verb to a noun and then tries to live from the *"place"* rather than from the *"movement"* of grace.

Across the globe there are museums which house creative works by artists gifted with talents from a generous Father. These works are monuments to a movement of creativity, nouns from a verb. Israel in the wilderness often had to confront this very process. They followed God's movement until it stopped. They would build the temple (noun) where it stopped and worshipped God in that place until they saw Him move (verb) again. When David desired to build a house for God, he modified the verb of God's presence towards a noun of God's habitation – he halted the Kingdom of grace to a place rather than a lifestyle. God still expects us to live *"by grace"* not *"in grace."*

How many of you are waiting for the next *"move"* of God or seeking for a past monument to a movement? Notice in this one question the verb/noun confusion which many have adopted. *"To wait"* is not a verb but a noun – you are a statue watching life pass you by until God decides to move! God is always moving which means grace is always moving too. *"To seek"* is what a verb represents – action. You move, overturn things, look around, constantly in motion trying to perceive movement. But seeking for something that looks like a past movement of God is not perceiving, it is recognizing. (I realize that you teachers out there will have much concern about what I just claimed about *"waiting"* not being a verb, but in my mind statues don't move. So just go along with the metaphor.)

John tells us that we do not know what Jesus will look like when he returns but that we will be like him. We will not recognize him. John also tells us that the angels circle the throne of grace saying *"Holy, Holy, Holy,"* as new revelation of God unfolds before them. If the angels can't stop to *"recognize"* God why do we believe that we can?

How often have you prayed, *"God give me more grace,"* and not seen much happen? Can you tell me what you were asking for? Chances are quite high what you really wanted was more patience. If our prayers can be confounded by the use of one term over another, is it possible that a verb can be considered a noun and thereby lose the property which distinguished it in the first place?

Let me ask you these questions: Are you saved by grace? If so, is grace a noun or verb to you? Do you know if your salvation is a noun or a verb? How would you shift from a noun to a verb?

SAVED BY GRACE

Before we jump into the meat of this matter I want you to realize the extent of what we're about to embark upon. Your confession which I chastised you about a few moments ago comes from a verse out of the book of Ephesians, second chapter.

> *Even when we were dead in sins, hath quickened us together with Christ, (by grace ye are saved;) (Ephesians 2:5)*

I want to direct your attention for a moment to the word *"saved"* in this verse. It is an important word throughout all of the New Testament writings. It is the Greek word, *"sōzō"* and according to Thayer's Dictionary it has the meaning of:

1) to save, keep safe and sound, to rescue from danger or destruction

1a) one (from injury or peril)

1a1) to save a suffering one (from perishing), i.e. one suffering from disease, to make well, heal, restore to health

1b1) to preserve one who is in danger of destruction, to save or rescue

1b) to save in the technical biblical sense

1b1) negatively

1b1a) to deliver from the penalties of the Messianic judgment

1b1b) to save from the evils which obstruct the reception of the Messianic deliverance

Most people, because of their confession, fall into the latter category of this definition, the *"1b"* grouping. This is where they reside and never move beyond it. They got their *"Get into Heaven free"* card and don't intend to make waves. They have never realized that they can, and are required to embrace the entire definition of this word if they expect to live within the Kingdom of God.

I believe the reason believers have not embraced the fullness of the term *sōzō* is because they have nominalized the nature of grace. If grace has been nominalized then *sōzō* must follow in like kind, since you can't have the fullness of one without the other. But what do I mean when I use the term *"nominalized?"*

Let me ask you a series of question first to set this in proper order. Can you describe what grace looks like when it's operating? How do you spot it in your daily activities? What characteristics does it have that lets you know it's working on your behalf? When grace is working for you, which one, or more of your senses, lock into its workings? Simply put: What evidence do you have to present that confirms you're walking in grace?

To nominalize something means you have taken its action and converted it into an object. For you English majors, you've made a verb into a noun. Your inability to answer the questions above without well founded examples based on palpable, tangible evidence, or without the result of an action, demonstrates how grace has been nominalized in your life. If grace has been nominalized, then your salvation has been also! (And you wonder why there is no power in your life.) This is why I admonished you about claiming to be a sinner saved by grace. The traditions of man have in your confession changed the verb to a noun.

What needs to be done now is acknowledge that your understanding of grace is sub-par. There is nothing wrong with admitting this even with all the teaching about it that you may have had to endure. Let's just accept that you need to advance to the next level and are open and willing to learn how to shift the noun back to its rightful place as a verb. So with this new insight let's go find out what the real meaning of grace is and reclaim the fullness of your salvation.

BASIC TRAINING

The holy canon of writings which we call the inspired Word of God is broken down into two distinct compilations; the Hebrew Scriptures, called the Old Testament, and the Greek Scriptures, called the New Testament. Today these two compilations have been assembled into one collection known as the Bible, a Greek word which means "book."

The Old Testament manuscripts are divided into three classes: 1. The Torah, consisting of the first five books written by Moses which describe the origins of the nation of Israel, its covenant with God and the laws of the covenant; 2. The Prophets, which details the historical conflicts that Israel had with the surrounding countries and the foreign gods those countries worshiped; 3. The Poetry writings, which includes the psalms and wisdom literature.

The New Testament manuscripts are divided into two classes: 1. The Gospels, four books which detail the life of Jesus; 2. The Epistles, letters written to various church congregations by the Apostles of the first century church.

This is the basics, right? So let me ask you a question: Is grace a New or Old Testament reality? Be careful how you answer this because you need to know if what you're about to say is what has been told to you or what you actually believe to be true. Circle your answer in the following statement.

Query: Grace is a New Testament / Old Testament reality.

The term *"grace"* will be found in the interpretations of the New Testament writings. Did you catch that or were you sleeping? Let me wake you up. Grace does not exist in the original New or Old Testament writings because *"grace"* is an interpretive word. What is an interpretive word?

An interpreter's job is to take the language from one country and convey it into the language of another country. Let me explain it in this manner. A common activity in the United States is to go and fill up a car with gas. This activity is also common in the nation of England, but they fill their cars with *"petrol."* Here are two countries, with the same language, yet both have different words for the same product. An interpretive word is what develops when trying to bridge similar terms from differing languages and cultures.

If you think this example a bit far-fetched consider the term *"gas"* which comes from the term *"gasoline,"* a flammable, liquid hydrocarbon mixture, which was first used back in 1865.[3] The term *"petrol,"* where we get the word *"petroleum,"* comes from a Greek word which means, *"rock oil,"* and its first recorded use was in 1546.[4] Yes, gasoline comes from petroleum, but depending on where you are standing, with a hose in your hand, determines on the *"interpretive word"* you will use to convey the deposit into your car.

When you pick up your Bible, you pick up a book. When you read from the book, you read an interpretation of the Hebrew and Greek script that these two compilations originally were written in. The word *"grace"* is a word to interpret the Greek word *"charis."* The English word of *"grace"* is an interpretation of the Latin word *"gratia."* Borrowing from the example above, do you think we fully understand grace enough to fuel our lives properly if it has already gone through two interpretations?

I could at this junction provide you with a list of definitions about the meaning of grace but would they be of any help if their interpretation wasn't from the original language of the Kingdom of

---

[3] Merriam-Webster Dictionary

[4] http://wiki.answers.com/Q/What_is_the_meaning_of_the_british_term_petrol

God? So rather than define it and build a catalogue of examples to back it up, let's take another route to understanding its meaning.

ORIGINAL MEANING

As an ambassador from the Kingdom of God it is my responsibility to interpret for you what *"grace"* means in your language so that we may be able to properly communicate with each other. Your present understanding of *"grace"* is based upon the content of meanings that have been placed within the word. Some of these may be correct, some may be close, and some may be completely off the mark.

Many of our denominations are interpretive words (i.e. Christian, Lutheran, Methodist, Quaker, Baptist, and Pentecostal) simply due to the traditions that began those movements and how they were "transcribed" to the general population through conversation. Let me ask you for a moment to suspend what your think you know from your traditions and allow me the opportunity to develop in you a kingdom perspective about the essence of this word you know as *"grace."* I'll begin doing that here.

> But when the fullness of the time was come, God sent forth his Son, made of a woman, made under the law, (Galatians 4:4)

The Kingdom of God is an eternal kingdom, meaning it has no reference to the duration of time – it knows no beginning and no end. In Galatians 4:4, Paul tells us that in the fullness of time, God sent his Son. The reference to time in this verse does not mean according to the clock of the Kingdom but to the clock of this world. Something happened in the timetable of Earth which set off an alarm in the eternal realm that caused Jesus to step into this world.

I want you to consider something for the moment: We pride ourselves on being the most advanced and civilized society ever to roam this planet; however, Jesus did not show up on our watch. Our great advances were not the trigger to activate the purposes of God in birthing a savior in the world. Our language, our customs, our worship, our devotion, and so much more, have evolved past the environment from the fateful day that Jesus expelled with His last breath, "...it is finished!"

I'm not looking at what was the trigger which caused Jesus to come on the scene. I'm more interested in what the scene looked like that enabled Jesus, and His message, to *"fit"* right in. Understanding the languages and customs in those days, from Rome to Jerusalem, will uncover a greater wealth of grace, giving us a far better appreciation in what the apostles used as their primary tool for raising up the first century church.

> *And the child grew, and waxed strong in spirit, filled with wisdom: and the* **grace** *of God was upon him. (Luke 2:40)*

> *And the Word was made flesh, and dwelt among us, (and we beheld his glory, the glory as of the only begotten of the Father,) full of* **grace** *and truth. (John 1:14)*

Luke tells us as He grew, Jesus had the *grace* of God upon Him. We see from John's account, when Jesus showed up, He was full of *grace* and truth. The passages from Luke and John have interpreted the Greek word *"charis"* into grace. However, there is this passage we need to look at too.

> *And Jesus increased in wisdom and stature, and in* **favor** *with God and man. (Luke 2:52)*

This follows our previous passage from Luke and note the word rendered as *"favor."* This is the Greek word *"charis"* too. At this point

I want you to recognize that Jesus had the *charis* of God upon Him as a child; grew in *charis* with God and man; and was full of *charis* and truth. I trust you're now seeing that there are dynamics to *"grace"* which may be hidden beneath the interpretations we've been saddled with. Let me bring these verses into play, also from John.

> *(16) And of his fullness have all we received, and grace for grace. (17) For the law was given by Moses, but grace and truth came by Jesus Christ. (John 1:16-17)*

John continues on about the fullness we have received from Jesus and also *charis* for *charis*. Then he declares that the law was given by Moses but *charis* and truth came, or better said, came into being or was fulfilled, by Jesus.

Jesus, the son of God, the Lord of Lords and King of Kings provides us with the proper example of not only what, but how, the Kingdom of God sees *"grace"*, *"charis"* or *"gratia"* represented. So in this book, whichever word I use - *grace*, *charis*, or *gratia* - they all hold the same meaning in the language of the Kingdom. My job will be to fill in the blank spaces so that they end up all having the exact same meaning when you use them.

Knowing *Charis*

> *For God pays no attention to this world's distinctions. . .*
> *For when Gentiles who have no Law obey by natural*
> *instinct the commands of the Law, they, without having*
> *a Law, are a Law to themselves; since they exhibit proof*
> *that a knowledge of the conduct which the Law*
> *requires is engraven on their hearts, while their*
> *consciences also bear witness to the Law, and their*
> *thoughts, as if in mutual discussion, accuse them or*
> *perhaps maintain their innocence – on the day when*
> *God will judge the secrets of men's lives by Jesus Christ,*
> *as declared in the Good News as I have taught*
> *it.(Romans 2:11,14-16)*

In this passage of scripture, there is no use of the word *"charis"* (pronounced *"Khar'-ece"*) and yet it describes what happens when a concept embodied in a social order has the ability to appear as a divine portrayal of the Kingdom of God. This is what I'll be discussing about the nature of *charis*.

Charis has a rich history in the Greek culture which predates the New Testament by a thousand years. Its concepts cannot easily be boiled down to one or two simple words or sentences which will properly portray the vast richness and complexities that this single word spans. Yet still we must begin somewhere in trying to convey the underlying essence of this word.

The entire New Testament writings are filled with the word *"charis"* since it occurs 156 times as twelve different interpretive words in the King James Version of the Bible. We have throughout much of church history assigned a meaning to this word (often not according the Greek mind-set) which has caused it to lose much of its character – not that this is bad, it's just not a complete picture. I want you to get re-acquainted with the word from the understanding of the early Greek poets as they used it in their writings. I hope to show how the ancient Greeks viewed the importance of this word in their daily lives and how it corresponds to passages in the Bible.

At this point I want to clear up any hesitation you may have about discussing the Greek culture in a book dedicated to the character of "grace." Grace is foundational to the New Testament writings which were transcribed into English from their original Greek. If we don't understand how the mind of a Greek reader thinks, which most of Western civilization if modeled after, how can we expect to truly know what Jesus and the Apostles were trying to communicate to people through their daily activities and conversations?

What is unique about *"charis"* is how the Apostle Paul, operating as an ambassador from the Kingdom of God, took this one Greek word, or concept, and through his writings single-handedly recast it, elevating it to an entirely new level of meaning. Today, unless you're a Greek scholar able to read New Testament Greek, you don't even recognize this and subsequently miss out on the deeper meaning of the text.

Charis today has an entirely different meaning than it had back "in the day." I want you to understand the word from how the poets and philosophers of "the day" understood and developed the character of the word. It was through their work that the social fabric of the Greeks culture was imparted with the understanding of *charis*.

The Age of Grace is a book written by Bonnie MacLachlan who has done a great study in the original meaning of *charis*. In her book, she provides excerpts from a number of works where Greek authors used *charis* within the context of the subject matter. She includes both the original Greek text and its translation to give you an understanding of the topic being covered. So what was *charis* to the early Greeks? In the introduction of Bonnie's book she states:

> "... No serious reader of early Greek poetry can avoid the fact that charis dominates the literary portrayal of life during the archaic age... Charis flickered when beautiful women sparkled; soldiers brought charis to their commanders on the battlefield or expected to win it when they fought well; charis graced appropriate behavior and speech and was a distinguishing mark of nobility; it was at the center of the feast; in the verses of the love poets it sat upon the hair or the eyes of the beloved. For the epinician poets it crowned the moment of supreme glory when the athlete won and was celebrated in song. Indeed, it would seem that for the early Greeks charis was present at all the high moments of life. And at death one faced the dreary prospect of the disappearance of charis. Just what was the charis experience, the sensation that clearly brought the greatest enjoyment to the early Greeks?"[5]

You can now see that *charis* as it was "back in the day" covered a lot of ground and I assure you, today, knowing this background as I do, the understanding that the church has about *grace/charis* is pretty pale in comparison.

RECIPROCAL IN NATURE

> "Some think that reciprocity is without qualification just, as the Pythagoreans said; for they defined justice without qualification as reciprocity. Now 'reciprocity' fits neither distributive nor rectificatory justice - yet people want even the justice of Rhadamanthus to mean this: Should a man suffer what he did,

---

[5] *The Age of Grace, Charis in Early Greek Poetry*, Bonnie MacLachlan, Princeton University Press, 1993

*right justice would be done - for in many cases reciprocity and rectificatory justice are not in accord; e.g. (1) if an official has inflicted a wound, he should not be wounded in return, and if some one has wounded an official, he ought not to be wounded only but punished in addition. Further (2) there is a great difference between a voluntary and an involuntary act. But in associations for exchange this sort of justice does hold men together - reciprocity in accordance with a proportion and not on the basis of precisely equal return. For it is by proportionate requital that the city holds together. Men seek to return either evil for evil - and if they cannot do so, think their position mere slavery - or good for good-and if they cannot do so there is no exchange, but it is by exchange that they hold together. This is why they give a prominent place to the temple of the Charites - to promote the requital of services; **for this is characteristic of charis - we should serve in return one who has shown charis to us, and should another time take the initiative in showing it.**"*
Aristotle, Nicomachean Ethics, Book 5

Aristotle declares the distinguishing characteristic of *charis* is reciprocity. Today we would know this process as The Golden Rule: Do unto others as you would have them do unto you. But how could this Greek society operate under such a clearly *"biblical"* order?

Consider that Greece is comprised of a main land and many islands which *"in the day"* were primarily agricultural. Each of these islands were inhabited by clans who were fiercely independent and yet socially dependent upon each other. Whenever a conflict would arise which would draw the men capable of fighting away from their homes, as a matter of social discourse, those who remained behind would tend to the estates of those who had gone on their behalf. This would create a bond within the societal order to insure the protection of the community not only in the present circumstance but also for future conflicts which might arise. Future generations were expected to fulfill their duty in honoring the sacrifices of those who had gone before them as an obligation to their own family's commitment to protect the interests of a neighbor.

This honoring of the obligations of a *"charis-event"* would be the glue that held the Greek society together for so many centuries. Some scholars even speculate the reason Greece never rose to a great economic power in the world was because of the rule of *charis* even in their business dealings.

What, you might ask, would happen if *charis* was not honored? In a societal structure so tightly interdependent upon one another, not honoring the *charis* which was extended to you by a neighbor was grounds for public humiliation and disgrace. It was acceptable practice to *"call out"* the offending party at any public gathering so as to insure that the community would be fully aware of the nature of the individual and how they conducted themselves with regards to commitments. In small communities this would be devastating to the person and their family for many generations afterwards since it would adversely affect their daily transactions within the community as well as virtually deprive them of any ability to protect their resources in any future conflict.

So we see here that *charis* has a specific nature associated with it which is evident in the actions of reciprocal exchange. This exchange process created a mechanism of honor which was passed down from generation to generation as reciprocal exchanges occurred within the social and economic fabric of each community. Eventually this pattern would become tarnished in the larger urban areas through the mechanism of political advantage and the buying of *"favors"* to extend and secure one's influence in the community. Yet in the rural areas, the operation of *charis* as it first developed would remain the *"law"* of the land.

My good buddy, Webster, has a dictionary which provides us with a better understanding of reciprocity when looking at the synonyms of mutual and common. *"Reciprocity"* implies an equal return or counteraction by each of two sides toward or against or in relation to the other; *Mutual* applies to feelings or effects shared by two jointly; *Common* does not suggest reciprocity but merely a sharing with each other."

In ordinary every day terms I'm going to reduce reciprocity to the concept of giving – you give something and you get something in return. Notice I said that I'm reducing it to this concept. *Charis* is much broader in scope, but we have to start somewhere with the intention that we'll build up from there. And what is a better place to start than with an action which everyone loves to benefit from? Tell me of a person who doesn't love getting a gift. I certainly do, and yes, I get great pleasure out of receiving them as I'm sure most of you do. Yet I want you to understand what I mean when I say *charis-pleasure* when talking about an act of *charis*. Bonnie MacLachlan describes this *charis-pleasure* as follows:

> *"Charis bound people together in the archaic Greek world, the experience of pleasure. Before the Greeks became citizens of a polis, when new and more complex levels of loyalty and obligation became operative, the distribution of favors and good behavior – such things that went by the name of charis – was enforced with a vigor that in unknown to us. We are familiar with charity that is voluntary and self-denying but, by the same token, was never confined to the self. The exchange of charis-favors was founded upon a very general psychological phenomenon, the disposition to return pleasure to someone who has given it. This pleasure exchange was accepted as a serious social convention... the charis-convention amounted to a lex talionis, but of a positive sort."[6]*

---

[6] *The Age of Grace, Charis in Early Greek Poetry*, Bonnie MacLachlan, Princeton

So let's look at this *charis-convention*. Reciprocity, the equal giving and taking of favors (or gifts according to our reduction of the concept) was a serious exchange of pleasure. I know that sounds a bit strange at first, but let me ask you this: Do you, or someone you know, get more pleasure out of giving a gift than receiving it? I know of a couple of people who get more wrapped up in the wrappings than in the receiving of the gift. And when I get something from them, I make it a point to make sure that I open it in front of them because half of my joy in the gift is watching how they respond to me opening it. Conversely, I know of a few people who love to get gifts and it's always a treat to watch them open a gift whether from me or anyone else.

Now notice that this *charis-convention* was social in nature. It never happened away in a closet, it was in front of people who would recognize its function. This means that the transaction had the ability to create a level of honor among the community who witnessed it. What I mean by this besides the obvious definition of honor, is that it set up an expectation of completion within the community by the nature of reciprocity. Example: Joe gives a gift to Ted while their friend Bill is watching. The exchange is marked by warm, sincere adoration. This exchange creates an expectation within Bill to see Ted return the gesture and even greater, Bill anticipates that Joe may extend to him a similar recognition.

I realize that some of you might take issue with the above example citing that it's too simple. This is intentional. I know that human dynamics in a social arena run in a myriad of directions, but this simple illustration shows the workings of *charis-pleasure* and the honor that *charis* establishes within relationships. There is pleasure in the giving and receiving of gifts – no one can deny this – yet there is an

University Press, 1993

expectation of honoring the reception of the gift which also comes with the transaction.

THE OLDEST GREEK EXAMPLE

In the opening pages of 1 Samuel we read the story of the two wives of Elkanah: Hannah, who was greatly loved, and Peninnah, who inflicted mental abuse upon Hannah since she was unable to bear a child. If you've done any Bible study you know that Hannah has a child which becomes Samuel, who eventually becomes the one who anoints David, Israel's greatest king, the forerunner to Jesus, the Messiah. What, you may ask, does all of this have to do with *charis* and the Greek culture?

I use this passage as a measuring tool since at this same time, several hundred miles to the north, on the northwestern edge of present day Turkey, a war is being fought; one which would last for ten years; a war that would become the defining moment for all of Greek society. It would shape the character of future national leaders like Alexander the Great who was to come almost 800 years after it had been fought. This war would be analyzed by great writers, poets, philosophers and military strategists for centuries, even up to this day. If the Red Sea was the defining moment for the tribe of Israel, this war, the Trojan War, was such a moment for Greece. Embodied within the backdrop of this conflict is the beginning of what we know of the nature of *charis*.

Before I go any further I want to emphasize something very important here in the context of this story. One of the oldest pieces of Greek literature which tells about this event was penned by Homer, and is called *The Iliad*. Homer wrote about this war over two hundred years <u>after</u> the events transpired, at about the time Solomon was dedicating the Temple of God in 1 Kings 7. Why is this important? The narrative of this ten year war was not penned by someone who witnessed it firsthand but by someone, who understanding the first nature of *charis*, was willing to bring, to as many as would receive it, honor where honor was due.

After this great war ran its course, as many had before it, champions and vanquished each went their way telling the stories of great battles and its heroes to all who would listen. Since they didn't have our modern conveniences of televised distraction, weekly, if not nightly, symposiums were the mainstay of the communal life and became the outlet for these stories.

Symposiums, unlike today's dry, staid intellectual forums were festive drinking events held after a communal feast where songs and stories of heroic deeds from the champions of the past and the present flowed as easily as the wine, which by its very nature, was the regulator on the ability of the teller to hold the attention of the audience. Over and over again these grand and noble stories would be told, each generation adding to the richness as new subjects of honor arose in the community. This is what we might call the oral traditions of a culture but to them it was an element of *charis* – giving honor to those who honor was due to.

Charis, in this venue, was something that every man acknowledged was important to the fabric of the community. Each man conducted his affairs so as not to be seen without honor, which could be brought up in these events just as well.

It is probable that the retelling of this great war always began with the phrase, "It was the face that would launch a thousand ships." This was the catalyst of the Trojan War, a ten year battle between the Spartans and the Trojans over Helen, said to be the most beautiful woman in all of the Earth and the wife of the Spartan King Menelaos, who was abducted by Paris the son of Priam, King of Troy.

Meneloas goes to his brother Agamemnon, the ruler of Mycenae and together the two try to diplomatically secure the return of Helen to her husband, without success. Meneloas decides to enlist the surrounding kingdoms in a campaign to rescue Helen and is joined by Nestor, an old family friend, in his journeys to solicit the aid of these kings and their armies.

Some scholars state that the reciprocity these kings show to Menelaos was a characteristic of the social order during the time recognizing how they would receive a portion of the spoil of the battles, while others suggest that many of them had been prior suitors of Helen and out of honor to her joined in this venture. Note now that these two thoughts, reciprocity and honor, are foundational to the Greek concept of *charis*.

One of those recruited by Nestor was Odysseus who had been warned that if he participated, his journey home would take him twenty years. He feigned madness until it was discovered the reason for his actions at which point he reluctantly enlisted his services. Many of the Greeks felt that they could not conquer Troy unless they employed the talents of the greatest warrior on the face of the Earth, Achilles.

Achilles had been warned that he would receive great glory in the battle but that he would die at a young age. His mother, subsequently hearing this, disguised him in woman's clothing, which was discovered by Odysseus. Achilles agreed to join the conquest much to the joy of many. An armada of over a thousand ships representing all the Achaian independent states aligned with Meneloas set sail from Sparta with Agamemnon chosen as their general.

The Iliad picks up the story of the battle in its ninth year and there is great turmoil in the Achaian camp due to a *charis-event* between Agamemnon and Achilles. Apparently Agamemnon withheld a portion of his rightful spoil from Achilles from a battle where he was clearly the victor and took Briseis, the concubine of Achilles, from his tent. This was conducted in full view of the Achaian army which enflamed the anger of Achilles to such a degree that he publicly denounced Agamemnon and pulled his entire army from the battlefront back to the boats declaring that he was returning the following day back to his home.

Meanwhile in Agamemnon's tent, Nestor is showing the council how Achilles departure is demoralizing the troops and Agamemnon needs to make amend with Achilles. He agrees that he has wronged Achilles and offers many gifts and riches to be presented to him and the return of Briseis as an offer of reconciliation. Odysseus and Ajax go to Achilles with the gifts and are welcomed into Achilles tent with great honor but he refuses to take the items or accept any terms which Agamemnon has to offer him with the following response:

"Nor do I think that Agamemnon son of Atreus nor the Danaans will persuade me, since there was no spoil (charis), then or now, for fighting against enemy-men, ever tirelessly." Il, 9.315-17

So incensed by what Agamemnon has done to him publicly, Achilles swears that even if all of the treasures of Egypt were given to him he still would not return to fight along side Agamemnon. He claims that all which had been promised and delivered to him did not constitute *charis* to him. This deeply concerns Odysseus who makes an impassioned plea with Achilles to reconsider since his absence is causing a great toll on the battlefield to the Achaians and there is a moral obligation that he owes to his comrades. Again, this argument fails because it too lacks *charis* for Achilles.

In this matter some distinctions should be made. Many might think, and have thought over the centuries, that Achilles is acting out from a wounding of his pride because of the dishonor which

Agamemnon displayed to him. These thoughts don't take into consideration Achilles main point: *Charis* is not present. We've seen already that *charis* deals with the aspect of honor and reciprocity, but in this instance the missing component is a "pleasure producing" aspect which has been severed from *charis*.

True, Agamemnon did trample upon the *charis-honor* of Achilles by taking the spoil and his concubine which rightfully belonged to him. True, there is reciprocity on the battlefield as warriors fight beside each other that insures a sense of safety as each watches out for the other in the heat of the conflict. But according to Achilles, the *charis-pleasure* which comes from obtaining the spoils and *charis-pleasure* that he as commander experiences when he and his troops successfully vanquish a foe has been taken from him by Agamemnon's actions.

Furthermore, it must be kept in mind here that the relationship which Agamemnon has with every member of this expedition. While he is the general, he is an equal with everyone in this battle. Each has the freewill to decide the course of his own actions on and off the battlefield. Achilles recognized that Agamemnon does not, by his very position as general, have a higher sense of responsibility which alleviates him from entering the battle while still enabling him to partaking of its spoils. This was what Achilles believed Agamemnon had embarked upon and it would cause division among the ranks of the men if they felt that their efforts might be undermined too, and this could spell defeat for the entire army if it was allowed to continue.

There is much more to the workings of this story that I could elaborate upon but I believe at this point you have been given the primary understandings of *charis* as the Greek population understood it "back in the day." What they recognized about *charis* was:

- It was an honoring event.

- It produced pleasure

- It was reciprocal

- It was demonstrated by a gift or favor.

- It was socially expected.

Each of these components became a belief structure in the Greek culture and happened long before David, the precursor of Jesus even came on the scene. I want you to consider this before we proceed: Of the 27 books canonized in the New Testament, eight are written to church congregants who could trace their ancestry back to at least the time of Aristotle; two books are written to an influential Greek benefactor who also could possibly trace his heritage back to Aristotle; three books are written to overseers of churches located in this same region where the Trojan war was fought and describe how drawing on the cultural history will impact the new believer; and one book was written to church congregants who had deposed the Greek empire, integrated its population, and become the ruling empire of the age.

This means that over 50% of the New Testament was addressing the Greeks and not in word form only. A simple reading of Luke's account of Paul's journeys recorded in the book of Acts clearly indicates that in many cases it wasn't the Jews who welcomed the gospel message but the populace with Greek heritage. This is why I have proceeded down this path. I have nothing against the Jews and their culture, they after all gave us the Messiah. In order to understand the importance of *charis*, or grace, we have to come at it from the Greek culture where its very operation was already ingrained in the societal structure.

Knowing what we do about what the Apostle Paul preached, what about it was so influential to a pagan culture that it eventually took over the entire region? Simple: Paul spoke about *charis*, or grace, which came from Heaven in the form of Jesus. It wasn't a Jewish Messiah who these listeners heard about; it was about the reciprocal nature of *charis*, or grace, in the exchange which Jesus made for them. They lived this reciprocal lifestyle in their community; their poets and philosophers had written about this nature of *charis*, or grace, for centuries, and now they were hearing how God was interacting with them on the same basis. Their own gods never conducted themselves in this manner – even the Charites who were known as "The Three Graces" never operated in this fashion! And now hearing this they experienced the foundational component of *charis*, or grace: Joy.

THE ROOT OF THE MATTER

When I speak about grace to most people there is this very somber mood which comes upon them as they relate to me their experiences of how grace has touched or affected their lives. At first I took this reverent tone as a mannerism of their experience, but recently I've become aware that this may be not the case. It is possible that the response is simply ignorance about the true nature of grace and what it produces. Before you go and get your dander up let me explain.

Grace, or *charis*, like most words, has a root word that it comes from. Root words are foundational in understanding the meaning of not only a word but how its use can be interpreted in its context. If you know the root you know how to properly advance the meaning of the word.

We've seen that the Greek word for grace is *charis*. This word comes from the root word *chara*. You'll discover its meaning in this passage of scripture.

> For the kingdom of God is not meat and drink; but
> righteousness, and peace, and joy (chara) in the Holy
> Ghost. (Romans 14:17)

Chara is defined as, 1) joy, gladness; 1a) the joy received from you; 1b) the cause or occasion of joy; 1b1) of persons who are one's joy. The interesting aspect of chara is that it too has a root word which it comes from. Chara comes from the word Chairo which is defined as, 1) to rejoice, be glad; 2) to rejoice exceedingly; 3) to be well, thrive; 4) in salutations, hail!; 5) at the beginning of letters: to give one greeting, salute. This word, chairo, can be found in this passage.

> Rejoice (chairo) in the Lord always: and again I say,
> Rejoice(chairo). (Philippians 4:4)

So what does all of this mean? Well any discussion about grace has to take into consideration the fact that whatever the meaning of grace is, its very foundation is built upon the nature of joy and rejoicing. This means there is a nature of pleasure associated with whatever grace means and this pleasure is expressive in a positive, joyful manner.

So why the frowns and sullen expressions whenever the matter of grace arises? Could it be ignorance about the basic joyous nature of grace? It seems most congregants have been indoctrinated that God stands over them with a bat and waits to clobber them at any moment they make the slightest mistake. This mindset has filtered out into the "world" through our daily discourse so that even our relationships with the "world" are tainted with frowns.

Consider that when you begin to smile you may actually be moving into the realm of grace more than you realize. The Old Testament clearly states that, ". . . Joy of the Lord is your strength." Now we can say that the foundation of grace, which is joy, is your strength. So where is this leading us?

> *But rather seek ye the kingdom of God; and all these things shall be added unto you. Fear not, little flock; for it is your Father's good pleasure to give you the kingdom. (Luke 12:31-32)*

From this point forward we are going to look at grace and the Kingdom with a mind that has been renewed in the nature of joy. So using this *"new"* thought about the nature of *charis*, let's go look elsewhere at how it shows up in the Bible.

Back In Time

Let me ask you a question. Do you know when grace began?

Most people have never thought about it. Why should you, after all you're saved by grace. You've got your "Get into Heaven free card."

Is it possible there could be something more important to the nature of grace than getting into Heaven? If the question has been asked, it's possible that looking into this matter may have ramifications upon your walk as a Christian believer.

So when do you think grace began? Was it when you accepted Jesus as Lord of your life? Or was it at His sacrifice on the cross? Or maybe it was in the garden of Gethsemane when He proclaimed *". . . not my will but Your will be done."* How about when He was born? With so many choices it's becoming evident that the beginning of grace could have a different impact on your life depending on where you view it. Fortunately the Bible has the answer for us.

> *Who hath saved us, and called us with a holy calling, not according to our works, but according to his own purpose and grace, which was given us in Christ Jesus before the world began (2 Timothy 1:9)*

There is the answer and probably not what you were expecting is it? When anything is defined as *"before the world began,"* you're talking about something which comes from an eternal realm. This means that grace is not trafficking in time, or in other words, there is never a time when grace did not exist. So even when you consider the times listed above, grace was even in operation at the creation of the world! This means that even when the man and the woman fell, grace was operating. But can you spot it working?

Probably not, since grace, as you know it, is a Greek term and you won't find it in a Hebrew-written Bible. If you know what the characteristics of *charis* are from a New Testament perspective then you'll be able to recognize it in the Old Testament writings.

"...before the world began..." is an important part of our entire discussion on grace since it gives us a means of determining *"time"*. The difficulty is that time, as we know it, is defined to a creation event which occurred on the fourth day as noted in Genesis 1:14.

> *And God said, Let there be lights in the firmament of the heaven to divide the day from the night; and let them be for signs, and for seasons, and for days, and years: (Genesis 1:14)*

So what is *"time"* called prior to Genesis 1:14? Eternity. In the first thirteen verses of Genesis the works which are being conducted are in the eternal realm, and according to 2 Timothy 1:9, grace is an eternal component of God's purpose. What significance is this to us? Let's take a look at this from a salvation perspective.

A point occurs where you make the decision to accept the Lordship of Jesus over your life. This point is defined by your recognition of having missed the mark (sinned) that God predestined for you. The only remedy is found in the work which Jesus accomplished for you. In keeping with my mission of driving the importance of the union between *"sōzō"* and *charis* I'm going to take you back once again to Ephesians 2:4-5.

But God, who is rich in mercy, for his great love wherewith he loved us, (5) Even when we were dead in sins, hath quickened us together with Christ, (by grace ye are saved;) (Ephesians 2:4-5)

Most people believe that their salvation follows a "cause and effect" mechanism: My sin (cause) separates me from God (effect); I accept Jesus (cause) and regain access to God (effect). The dilemma with this thinking is that most people who prolong their salvation decision do so because they don't believe they have done anything in their life prior to the salvation moment which can be viewed as *"sin."* They are looking for a *"time"* in their life when they committed something wrong (cause) which would require them to turn to Jesus (effect). **Cause and effect mechanisms are bound in time events.**

Do you understand what I just said? Every effect is a result traveling over a span of time from some cause. Everything which occurs in a dimension of time is a result of something which transpired prior to the event in the same time dimension. Dimensions of time have a starting point (cause) and an ending point (effect). Life on this planet is one big cause and effect scenario being played out with billions of people. **However, grace isn't a component of this time dimension – it is eternal.** This means that your salvation *"by grace"* is not based upon any previous time-based event (cause).

But we are time-based creatures right? How can salvation not be a "cause and effect" mechanism? The answer is found in Romans 6:23.

For the wages of sin is death; but the gift of God is eternal life through Jesus Christ our Lord. (Romans 6:23)

Death, you've got to admit, is a time-based element. We call the beginning of something bound in time as the *"birth"* while the end of the same thing as *"death."* So let me ask you a couple of questions:

1) Have you died in Christ? 2) Are you born again? Notice in both of these *"salvation"* questions a reference is made to a time-event in the words *"died"* and *"born"*. What does this have to do with Romans 6:23?

The gift of God is *"eternal"* life. The gift is not bound by time. There is no beginning or end of the gift. The time-dimensional characteristic of eternity is that it is always *"now"*. The gift of eternal life is always now. Get ready for this: The word *"gift"* in this verse, its Greek root meaning is *"charis"*. The *"grace-gift"* from God is eternal life. Your salvation is an ending of a life bound in time and a new-birth into an eternal realm where there is no death. This is your grace-gift from God: a life like His.

So here are a couple of questions to ponder: 1) Why are you allowing a time-based event (death) still dictate your actions on this world? 2) If you are *"saved,"* when does eternal life start for you, at your birth or death?

STILL BEFORE

I'm not done with *"...before the foundation..."* in this matter. Let's consider what else was *"before"* since it plays a role in recognizing how grace operates.

> But we speak the wisdom of God in a mystery, even the hidden wisdom, which God ordained before the world unto our glory: (1 Corinthians 2:7)

We find here that the wisdom which we speak from the Kingdom was already established and put in place *"...before the world..."*and this eternal wisdom is for our glory. (For those of you who have taken a vow of austerity, glory is one of those good things you'll need to be wary of in order to keep up appearances.)

According as he hath chosen us in him before the foundation of the world, that we should be holy and without blame before him in love: (5) Having predestinated us unto the adoption of children by Jesus Christ to himself, according to the good pleasure of his will, (Ephesians 1:4-5)

Here we find that God planned for us to be holy and blameless, having chosen us and adopting us in Jesus Christ *"...before the foundation of the world..."*and this was done because it *"pleased"* Him.

In hope of eternal life, which God, that cannot lie, promised before the world began; (Titus 1:2)

The promise of eternal life, as I've stated earlier, was made *"...before the world began..."*

Forasmuch as ye know that ye were not redeemed with corruptible things, as silver and gold, from your vain conversation received by tradition from your fathers;(19) But with the precious blood of Christ, as of a lamb without blemish and without spot:(20) Who verily was foreordained before the foundation of the world, but was manifest in these last times for you. (1 Peter 1:18-20)

And let's not forget the matter of the lamb foreordained and slain *"...before the foundation of the world..."* I need to bring a vital point out here. The word "foundation" conjures up in the minds of most people a structure that is buried in the earth that a building is erected upon. While this is correct, it is not the picture which is being portrayed in these passages of scripture when you place the word "before" in front of it.

What the original language conveys is the process of conceiving, designing and planning a project before any material is placed in, or rises up from the ground. This is the process an architect or engineer goes through in creating a building or community; a craftsman operates from in creating any new piece of art or furniture. Here, in the operation of grace, is where all the details are addressed - the interconnectedness of it all - across a multitude of expanding possibilities.

Each of the items (i.e. wisdom, eternal life, and adoption as son, holy and blameless) has been thought out, planned and executed for us in the eternal realm by the Master Architect before any creation event occurred. They are to be manifested in this world by us as an act of the planning of Kingdom of Grace.

KINGDOM OF GRACE

Not many people have ever heard the term *"Kingdom of Grace."* I believe this is due to a lack of understanding about the operation of God's Kingdom as described in the Bible. If you're going to begin any discussion on God's Kingdom, then we have to begin at the required scripture, Matthew 6:33.

> *But seek first the kingdom of God and His righteousness,*
> *and all these things shall be added to you.*

Jesus, speaking in this verse, is pretty clear about what is important. So let me ask you something: When you think about what a kingdom looks like, what do you envision? Is it dominion, lands, castles, wealth, abundance? That's good but it's not complete yet. Certainly, every kingdom has a king and he wears a crown; land comes with being a king; yes, there are housing obligations which come with being a king; and there certainly is all that abundance the territory produces on behalf of the king, but there is one item that every kingdom has that most people overlook:

> *Let us therefore come boldly to the throne of grace, that we may obtain mercy and find grace to help in time of need. (Hebrews 4:16)*

A throne is the point where all power and authority is administrated by a king. It identifies the nature and realm of the king. I need to make an important point here. The power of the kingdom is not in the appearance of the throne, but what is administrated from that throne.

Recall the matter about nominalization of a word in the beginning of this book. Many believers have done this to the throne of God's Kingdom. It is as if they have made a *"throne of gold"* have the same meaning as a *"throne of grace."* Gold is always a noun, and grace will always be a verb! It is the actions that are transpiring from this throne which are being designated as *"grace,"* not the composition of the throne itself.

In Isaiah we are told the Messiah will rule from the throne of David. Here in Hebrews we are told to go boldly to the throne of grace. If you know anything about how a kingdom operates, no one can boldly approach a throne unless they have been declared by the king to be in *"right standing"* with him. The official term is: righteous.

If you are righteous in this Kingdom, coming and going boldly from before the throne, is acting in a manner that is called *"grace."* Now we get to round out our picture from the verse in Matthew 6:33. The operation of God's Kingdom from its throne is distinguished by actions of grace. We boldly go before the throne because we're righteous. What's that, you don't know about the righteous part?

For He made Him who knew no sin to be sin for us, that we might become the righteousness of God in Him. (2 Corinthians 5:21)

Well lookie there, God took care of that for you too! If you're in Jesus then you have God's righteousness, and it's pretty important to Him because in order for grace to operate, you, me, anybody for that matter, has to have righteousness. This is your introduction to the Kingdom of Grace. It has always been there — you just possibly didn't recognize it.

KINGDOM MATTERS

According to Ephesians 1:4 you and I were in Christ before the foundation of the world. We were then, and are today, kingdom citizens. You and I have been reunited in Christ through our belief in what He accomplished for us at the cross and upon His resurrection. Today, we occupy a place in Heaven right next to the throne of grace while we also traffic on Earth. This dual occupancy marks us as ambassadors from the Kingdom of Heaven.

Kingdoms transact with other kingdoms through covenant agreements. These agreements are administrated by the sovereign who made them and the sovereign demands that all the citizenry adhere to their requirements or face punishment for their disobedience to the agreement. If there is a transgression, the offender can appeal only to the sovereign for clemency. It is at this point you need to be introduced to a new set of terms and their attending concepts to round out this discussion. In what follows we will look at mercy and the Hebrew word *chesed* to see how they interact with grace.

Hebrew to Greek
and Back Again

I wrote the following in *Chesed – Beyond the Veil of Mercy:*

As we go into this study it would help to know where we're at presently with the definition of "mercy." Most people have adopted the definition which Webster's goes by:

That benevolence, mildness or tenderness of heart which disposes a person to overlook injuries, or to treat an offender better than he deserves; the disposition that tempers justice, and induces an injured person to forgive trespasses and injuries, and to forbear punishment, or inflict less than law or justice will warrant.

This is the customary definition which we've all embraced, saved and unsaved alike, over the generations. When I talk about the veil of mercy, this definition, its characteristics, its actions, reactions, and its presupposition are what I'm referring to. But the meaning behind any language evolves over time, so we need to get back to the original substance of the words if this study is going to make any sense.

But God, who is rich in mercy, because of His great love with which He loved us, (5) even when we were dead in trespasses, made us alive together with Christ (by grace you have been saved)...(12) That at that time ye were without Christ, being aliens from the commonwealth of Israel, and strangers from the *covenants of promise, having no hope, and without God in the world: (13) But now in Christ Jesus ye who sometimes were far off are made nigh by the blood of Christ. (Ephesians 2:4-5, 12-13)*

You may have read these verses a number of times but I can assure you that when we're done, the word "mercy" in verse 4 will have a greater significance then you've ever thought possible and change the whole meaning to this passage.

The original text which Paul wrote all his letters in was Greek, a language which for almost 400 years was the standard for all communications in the region. The covenants of promise which Paul speaks about were contained in the Hebrew writings of Moses and the Prophets.

Recall the ending passage in Ephesians 2:4-5 uses the term "mercy." This word in the Greek is "eleos" and according to Thayer's Greek Definitions this word means:

mercy: kindness or good will towards the miserable and the afflicted, joined with a desire to help them

This definition is a starting point for understanding the term "mercy" however you need to understand that this definition by Thayer and the one which we've accepted from Webster at the beginning of this chapter are accurate and appropriate – if you're Greek!

"Eleos" is not an accurate description for a Hebrew thought which revolves around covenant, but I'm getting ahead of myself. When the scholars interpreted the Torah they were faced with a dilemma – one that every person faces when conveying a word from one language into another. What do you do if the language which you're translating into doesn't *have a word that exactly expresses the same meaning or doesn't even have a word? Or consider this: How do you convey an ancient concept to a new generation three millennium from when it was practiced? Making this relevant to your life: How would you explain an IPad to your great-grandparents back in the day when they were your age? The scholars had to choose the best word which most properly described what they were trying to get across.*

"Wait a minute! These scholars were only working with the Torah. Paul's writings are New Testament, 300 years later! Why does what Paul say in the New Testament have anything to do with the Old Testament writings?"

Consider this aspect for a moment. If you take a glass and fill it to the top with ice cubes you will be able to say that the glass is full, but you know it isn't. The shape of the cubes doesn't conform precisely to the shape of the glass. This leaves voids in the contents of the glass. Over time, if you leave the glass alone, the ice will melt and filling in the voids but the level of the contents will drop below the top of the glass. After this time span, people become more concerned with the contents rather than the container.

The glass in this example represents the Hebrew thought in a word while the ice cubes represent the Greek word for this thought. What those scholars established as the words for the Torah also carried over with the writings of the Prophets and the Wisdom Literature eventually covering all the Hebrew writings. Over time these words conformed to the Hebrew thought, but they didn't convey the full meaning, and people became more concerned about what the Greek word conformed to rather than the Hebrew thought which it was intended to convey.

Why should this matter? Recall that I stated we don't know anything about the covenants of hope and promise as the Hebrew people do just as Paul was reminding in the church in Ephesus too. The difference between the Greek understanding of "mercy" and the Hebrew understanding of "mercy" hinges on their relationship with God.

The Greeks never had a covenant with any of their gods, so how they viewed "mercy" has always been from a judgmental position. Even today this is still conveyed in the definition which we have adopted for "mercy." However, the Hebrew knowledge of "mercy" comes from a relationship established by covenant with God. Its meaning is entirely different because of this relationship.

Whether it's Hebrew into Greek or Hebrew into Greek and then into English, there is not a specifically accurate word which properly conveys the full meaning that the Hebrews had for this term we have called "mercy." It's time to find out what the real meaning is.

The heart of the matter

Recall from the previous chapter I mentioned the Greek word "eleos" is defined as "mercy." When the scholars made their translation of the Torah, they took the following Hebrew word and tried to fit it into the Greek word "eleos." (I'll let you determine later if they made the best choice.)

Chesed (Strong #2617) kindness, favour, good deeds, kindly, loving kindness, mercy, merciful, faithfulness

Chesed is one of the most important words in the Hebrew text being used almost 250 times; its depth of meaning cannot be contained in a single word. Actually, there is not an English word which can convey its full meaning.

A Starting Point

According to the Hebrew mystics – the rabbis and scholars who have spent their lives intensely studying the scriptures and the meaning behind all the words and letters – "chesed" is the beginning of all things. We live in a cause/effect environment. There is not one thing which you can do that does not have a corresponding response later. Throw a rock and its intersection with a pond, window or pack of dogs will create an effect. The mystics believe that "chesed" is the original spark – the kind deed – which God employed to start the cause and effect of creation. Today, it is through the employment of kind deeds which they believe the original spark is imparted to mankind thereby bringing the nature of God once again to man.

Now there is a vital distinction to this kind-deed principle which is important to grasp. In the Hebrew culture there are two classes of deeds: Tzedekah deeds and chesed deeds. Tzedekah, meaning righteous, are deeds that are performed because the Torah commands it be done if you are to remain faithful to the traditions of the Fathers. Each person recognizes that by doing these deeds (i.e. visiting the sick; caring for a widow; feeding the hungry) they can expect these same deeds to be performed for them should a time occur when they are grappling to survive through an experience.

Chesed deeds are more in alignment with the nature of God in that they are done without thought of the reward of a future compensation. In this manner they express a kindness or goodness in the person performing the deed which seeks to be more like God in His creating nature where chesed established for mankind an environment to thrive within.

Links observed

The Hebrew mystics further depict the relationship of chesed with two other concepts: justice and compassion. If you were to view each of these three on a continuum, chesed would appear on the right and act in an expansive nature; justice would appear on the left and act in a restrictive nature; while compassion would reside in the middle acting as the governor between the two extreme natures.

Another way to look at this would be to view a king sitting on his throne. In his right hand is chesed, kind deeds which he eagerly hands out in abundance to the members of his realm. In his left hand is his justice which he applies to reign in those who have extended themselves beyond the mandates of his kingdom. Independently, each can go to extremes in their employment, yet seated in the center, is the heart of a compassionate king who wisely balances the matters of chesed and justice.

You will also find on this continuum the position of mercy and forgiveness. Both appear on each side of compassion: forgiveness to the right, or chesed side, and mercy on the left, or the side of justice. Unlike the extreme positions which chesed and justice can travel, forgiveness and mercy remain stationary next to compassion. Using the example from above, mercy and forgiveness are the lungs which express the will of the compassionate heart. Mercy will always tend to have an element of justice involved with it, while forgiveness is the first expression of chesed revealed in compassion.

Chesed is the quality exercised mutually among equals; it is the kindliness of feeling, consideration and courtesy, which adds a grace and softness to the relationship between members of the same society.[7][8]

Let me clear up something here. The previous material might give the impression that I don't think there is any mercy in the Kingdom. This is the farthest thing from the truth. Let me try to explain what may be confusing to some, by picking up where I ended in the previous chapter.

You and I were in Christ before the foundations of the world. We were Kingdom citizens operating in the auspices of grace and *chesed*. After the Earth was created, a man, with the life force of God, was placed upon it to steward the garden. The relationship of grace and *chesed* was still in effect. When man fell, grace and *chesed* were broken, and man's dominion was lost. Man was placed into the mercy of the Creator.

Man, having been created in, and having operated from the environment of grace and *chesed*, determines to replicate this environment on his own, even though he is operating under mercy. Out of compassion, God makes a series of covenants with man in order to bring the environment of *chesed* back into the Earth. Through these covenants a shadow of the nature of grace is present but not apprehended, since sacrifices must be made yearly to address the requirements of a merciful God.

When Jesus came onto the scene, the fullness of grace and *chesed* returned to the Earth. The sacrificial exchange which Jesus made at the cross answered forever all the requirements of a merciful God and secured His forgiveness for all mankind. It also restored the

---

[7] *Hesed in the Bible,* Glueck, Wipf and Stock Publishers, 1967

[8] *Chesed – Beyond the Veil of Mercy,* mike hillebrecht, Charis Academy Publishing, 2012

---

environment of grace and *chesed* for mankind through the belief in the works of Jesus.

A believer operates not from mercy, but from *chesed*, because of the covenant that Jesus has made. As we move in Him, we function in His grace which was exchanged for the grace we created on our own. This grace exchange unites us as ambassadors from the Kingdom of God.

A non-believer still operates under mercy and a man-made grace, having lost the benefits of *chesed*. He will always appeal for mercy from God up until the day he believes in what Jesus accomplished for him. On that day, as a born-again believer, *chesed*, not mercy, is how life is conducted in the Kingdom.

The following gives us a path to follow from mercy to grace.

1.   In a kingdom, our posture determines our position. Our ego determines our position – are you trying to make a point or be the point.

2.   You don't remind a king of his position for his sake, but for your own sake. Thanksgiving and praise are evidence of your posture. Greatness never needs affirmation to be great. We need to recognize greatness and express gratitude for being next to it. Proximity to position demands recognition.

3.   Grace is easy to recognize when you're not in it. Everything that leads to the success of a king completing his purpose is the environment of grace.

4.   Mercy is the response of grace. A king can muscle his way around you - this is his right from his position of authority. Any response which differs from "muscling" is mercy given to a lack either in skill, intelligence, or position.

5. The purpose of mercy is to move you into grace. Any instruction from a king that enhances our capabilities in his court is intended to move us into his grace and experience the fullness of that environment from his perspective. Mercy continues to flow until grace is reached in every area of our lives.

6. The result of grace is relationship. Being a friend with a king means that you both operate in grace one to another. Mercy isn't offered to equals – being righteousness enacts chesed, from which grace is witnessed.

RENEWING THE MIND

Many believers have a hard time accepting what I just explained simply because they are stuck in their sin consciousness. This type of thinking doesn't recognize the potential of the new creation they have been made into. This is why the Apostle Paul admonishes us to renew our minds. The old pattern of thoughts, and their corresponding actions, must be eliminated by coming into an understanding of the truth of what was accomplished at the death and resurrection of Jesus.

There is a purpose for what God has done. If you don't understand that purpose how can you expect to receive the benefits He wants to extend to you? It's time to look at the purpose found above in item 6.

GRACE IS ABOUT RELATIONSHIPS

I want to bring to your attention a scripture that I believe is the most perfect example of the environment of grace you will ever witness in the entire Bible.

The grace of the Lord Jesus Christ, and the love of God, and the communion of the Holy Ghost, be with you all. Amen. (2 Corinthians 13:14)

This passage is the closing to the last letter which the Apostle Paul wrote to the church in Corinth. Some may see this as just a standard, if not noble, closing to a letter which at first glance would appear that way, yet Paul, from all of the letters which he wrote, only used this closing here. So I think the term "standard" doesn't truly fit the example. If you've just written an extensive letter to a body of people which commends them for their activities and faithfulness, wouldn't you want it to end on a high note, something that would hold their attention or bring it to remembrance at a later date? This is what we find here.

In this verse we find a number of elements that describe the environment which fosters the presence of grace according to the Greek mind-set, yet we also see the fullness of the Godhead associated with those various aspects in this environment. While the term *"environment"* does portray the inner workings of a set area adequately, it is a rather harsh, stifling word devoid of any real *"life"* and would probably work if I was writing this material for the scientific and research community. Since I'm not doing that, the more appropriate term would be captured in the word *"relationship"* and it is from here where we will delve into the heart of the matter.

WHAT MAKES FOR GOOD RELATIONSHIPS?

There are a number of well written authors out there who can expound on what makes for a good relationship among any type of people group. Yet in this passage we uncover the three aspects which are vital to every relationship. They are grace, love and communion. In the Greek these are *charis*, *agapē* and *koinōnia*. The English rendition of these words belittles the synergy that they exhibit in the Greek culture and it is my hope here that I will be able to bring this nature to life here for you. Since this is a study on grace, or *charis* in

Greek, I'll leave this one for the last. So I'll start with love or *agapē* in the Greek.

AGAPE

Love, as the song goes, is a many splendored thing. Paul associates love with God, the Father, and John brings this out in the following passage.

> *Beloved, let us love one another: for love is of God; and every one that loveth is born of God, and knoweth God. (8) He that loveth not knoweth not God; for God is love. (9) In this was manifested the love of God toward us, because that God sent his only begotten Son into the world, that we might live through him. (10) Herein is love, not that we loved God, but that he loved us, and sent his Son to be the propitiation for our sins. (11) Beloved, if God so loved us, we ought also to love one another. (1 John 4:7-11)*

In the Greek culture they have several words that describe love. Many of their poets and philosophers wrote and expounded extensively on love shown to a brother or the love between a man and woman. *Agapē* never shared the limelight in these writings and it wasn't until Paul, John, and the other New Testament writers began to incorporate it into their material that it began to receive any eminence. *Agapē* came to represent the highest form of love that one could offer. Strong's Concordance defines *agapē* as, "love, that is, affection or benevolence; specifically (plural) a lovefeast: – (feast of) charity ([-ably]), dear, love." It is in this definition that we begin to uncover an element which represented the early church activities and shed some light on part of Paul's first address to the Corinthians.

LOVE FEASTS

In Acts 2 we come across the origin of what would later be called *"love feasts."*

> *And they continued stedfastly in the apostles' doctrine and fellowship, and in breaking of bread, and in prayers... (46) And they, continuing daily with one accord in the temple, and breaking bread from house to house, did eat their meat with gladness and singleness of heart, (47) Praising God, and having favour (charis) with all the people. And the Lord added to the church daily such as should be saved. (Acts 2:42, 46-47)*

The daily breaking of bread from house to house is what we call today *"the house church movement."* It was the early believer's community structure which enabled them to pass along the apostle's doctrine and meet the needs of all who came under their influence. In the Greek language and culture this feasting or eating together is what is known as agapē. Now I don't want you to get the idea that these were elaborate dinners with multitudes of different foodstuffs because they often weren't at the beginning. They simply came together at the end of a busy day, bringing simple ingredients together and partook of the food which had been prepared. Bread and wine were integral elements since they represented to the followers the last supper of Jesus with his disciples.

What I find so interesting about these gatherings is that Saul, prior to his conversion and changing his name to Paul, used these feasts to determine where the *"church"* was meeting and subsequently persecute the followers of Jesus before the religious leaders of the day. It was Saul's persecution of *"love"* which would force the church out of Jerusalem into the *"world"*. The irony of all this is that Paul would provide directions in his first letter to the church at Corinth about how to conduct themselves during these *agapē* meals. They were following the extravagant manner of their past customs in conducting these feasts which left many, especially those who were not able to bring food, hungry upon their completion. The corrections Paul gave them would ultimately allow all the believers to experience the fullness of *agapē* in their community.

A crucial note in the history of these feasts occurred around 363-364 AD, when the Council of Laodicea passed an edict that forbade any church from celebrating an agape feast. The feast during this time had become an evening supper of "charity" to the people attending where the sacraments would be offered to all as part of the meal. Even three hundred years later it would be addressed by the Quinsext Council of 692 A.D. and its practice would eventually disappear in the churches. I find it amazing that *"the church"* would outlaw the very pillar of its creation, the very symbol which, according to our opening passage, associates love to God. Why any church would think it can practice its creed without the author of it is beyond me.

KOINONIA

Whenever people come together, whether it is at a meal or at a present-day church service, the one thing you should be looking for is *koinōnia* or what we more commonly call *"fellowship."* Another term that can be used here is *"communion"* and it possibly has the closest understanding to what *koinōnia* is trying to describe. Communion, or common union, indicates oneness in spirit, mind and communication. It is the essence of any lasting partnership. We have all had experiences where our communication with others has been *"out of sorts"* while at other times it may have been *"in sync."* These instances demonstrate the effect that *koinōnia* has on our interaction with others.

The Holy Spirit is associated with *koinōnia* in Paul's passage, meaning the Holy Spirit is the overseer of our fellowship with the Father. Jesus said the Holy Spirit would be our comforter, counselor and teacher, and that He would not speak on His own authority but would tell us of those things to come. These functions are vital to maintaining fellowship with the Father. Through the leading of the Holy Spirit we are taught how to function correctly in God's Kingdom as a son and heir. The Holy Spirit shows us how to properly communicate and follow the protocol which the Kingdom operates under so we can remain in common union with other believers and the Father. Our example in this would be Jesus where He declared He only did those things that He saw the Father doing. There is the *"oneness"* that Jesus prayed for us to possess in John 17; this oneness is the essence of *koinōnia*.

CHARIS

You're at an event which exudes love among the participants and there are obvious displays of affection and camaraderie. You are experiencing *agapē* and *koinōnia* in their fullest forms. As you experience this you will start to witness the manifestation of *charis*, or grace, between the participants. I've already explored the foundational characteristic of grace in its nature of reciprocal giving, as well as its ability to produce joy. In the presence of *agapē* and *koinōnia*, *charis* raises to a whole new level that can best be categorized as *"life-giving."* If you've ever been a member of a group that whenever they met there was something which inspired you to be and give all you could for *"the cause"*, you have experienced the elevated effect of grace from a position of man. Take this to the level of the Kingdom of God and it becomes personified as Jesus, the ultimate life-giving gift of God.

Paul clearly designates Jesus' work as the *"grace-gift"* in this relationship of the Godhead, a result of the love of the Father who seeks to bring communion with everyone through the Holy Spirit. If you take just one of these elements away, then the whole thing falls apart. Each of these three, *charis*, *agapē* and *koinōnia* are dependent upon, and the result of their interaction with, each other. Remove the elements of love and people have no reason to extend a gift to another; take away the fellowship and there is no one to give to; and take away the joy of giving and you end up with religion.

So in this one passage we see the ultimate depiction of the relationship of the Godhead and how we are to mirror this same relationship one with another as a model of the Kingdom of God working in our lives. If we can ever get beyond the differences we focus on and regain the sight of the purpose of the Father we just might witness the power that comes from living a life of grace, the same power the first church lived daily.

The Pleasure of Grace

Okay, we've spent a little time being introduced into the wonders of grace. It's time to now go deeper and begin exploring the many facets that enabled the New Testament writers to communicate with a culture which understood the fullness of grace as it resided on the Earth. Yes, this statement implies that there are at least two types of grace: The grace of man, and the grace of the Kingdom of God. Many don't understand this and think that there is only one. Unfortunately, you can't live from the Kingdom of God employing the grace of man.

> But rather seek ye the kingdom of God; and all these things shall be added unto you. (32) Fear not, little flock; for it is your Father's good pleasure to give you the kingdom. (Luke 12:31-32)

Reciprocity, according to Aristotle, is the primary characteristic displayed in *charis*, or grace. The Greek mindset to reciprocity held great social meaning. This is what Paul and Luke would draw upon in their dialogues with the churches in their day. In today's language we don't use the term *"reciprocal"* much to explain social discourse. If you wanted to get into a more relevant term which portrayed the transaction between the parties we could use *"exchange."* But our most frequently used term which conveys the appropriate symbolism is primarily *"give"* or *"gave"*.

Recall that the root meaning of grace is joy. So tying this together with reciprocity we should see that grace is joyful giving. This is a concept which is pretty transparent even in our daily lives. Who doesn't enjoy giving a gift? Obviously, we more often enjoy receiving gifts more than giving them, but this aside, the pleasure which comes from the transaction of giving is what the early Greeks recognized as an operation of grace. If this was true for the Greeks, then it should be reflected in scripture in other locations also. Well, here are a few of the more memorable verses where this concept appears.

> *Every man according as he purposeth in his heart, so let him give; not grudgingly, or of necessity: for God loveth a cheerful giver. (2 Corinthians 9:7)*

> *For God so loved the world, that he gave his only begotten Son, that whosoever believeth in him should not perish, but have everlasting life. (John 3:16)*

> *Having predestinated us unto the adoption of children by Jesus Christ to himself, according to the good pleasure of his will, (Ephesians 1:5)*

> *Having made known unto us the mystery of his will, according to his good pleasure which he hath purposed in himself: (Ephesians 1:9)*

In these passages we see that there is a nature of pleasure the Father demonstrates in His activities with us. This is a result of the dimension of grace which surrounds and emanates from His throne. Don't get me wrong here: The Father is not demonstrating pleasure simply from a position of authority. This would be like saying that you're only pleased with your kids when you can control what their interaction is with you. Pleasure is as fundamental with the nature of the Father as it is with us: He has made it a visible component of His realm and this is reflected in His purposes. This even applies where we least expect it.

> Yet it pleased the LORD to bruise him; he hath put him to grief: when thou shalt make his soul an offering for sin, he shall see his seed, he shall prolong his days,and the pleasure of the LORD shall prosper in his hand. (Isa 53:10)

Isaiah is speaking of events which would occur when the ruling powers of the region would be operating with Greek understanding. Isaiah's language reflects what he was seeing prophetically in the future. Even a casual reader of the Bible has difficulty with this passage when you speak of pleasure being derived from beating someone. Recognize this "pleasure" is coming from a realm where the authority and judgments made are based upon a purpose that pleases the sovereign in a reciprocal manner. The transaction, or exchange, conducted in this verse by the bruising, returns a prosperous, prolonging of days which pleases the Lord.

So now appreciating this matter of the pleasure of grace, its reciprocal nature, and the joy in giving, let's see what you can get when you add this verse.

> I have shewed you all things, how that so labouring ye ought to support the weak, and to remember the words of the Lord Jesus, how he said, It is more blessed to give than to receive. (Act 20:35)

Tell me if this sounds familiar. You've been invited to a party given by a distant relative who you've never been really close to. A couple of hours prior to the party you're told that an aunt of yours will be attending the same party. This aunt has always been the type to pour out gifts to everyone no matter what the occasion and you've been the proud recipient of a number of her gifts over the years. While it had never been your intention to bring a gift, now you feel obligated to bring a gift to *"offset"* the gift you know she will have for you. The circumstances may be different but the feeling of *"offsetting"* is what you always experience. Welcome the nature of reciprocal giving.

Mankind has always felt the obligation to return a gift, or favor, from someone who is close to them; or in a position where they might have an influence in their life, like a boss, business associate, politician, or the like. Actually this form of reciprocal giving of favors and gifts is what the ancient Greek society had evolved to by the time Aristotle wrote his treatise declaring that grace was distinguished by reciprocal giving. During that time, and even up until the Apostle Paul, the Greek culture was structured in such a manner that in order to obtain any position of influence, it was expected for one to give, or work, towards the favor of a benefactor who could place them into the position of influence which was being sought. This process of obtaining favor from a benefactor was known as *"charis,"* the very word that is transcribed as *"grace"* in the New Testament. Now being aware of this facet of grace, you may be able to comprehend what Paul is stating in this passage.

> *For by grace you have been saved through faith, and that not of yourselves; it is the gift of God, (9) not of works, lest anyone should boast. (Ephesians 2:8-9)*

Paul is conveying to the people of Ephesus that the nature of grace which saves them is the nature *charis* really had all those years prior to Aristotle. In the early days of the Greek social structure reciprocal giving was conducted as a means of ensuring the survival of the community when danger became present.

The important factor in this transaction was that no one was compelled to return the favor immediately. It was understood that this form of grace was generational in nature, meaning the return of the favor may not be needed to be returned until the next threat appeared which might not happen for several decades or even a lifetime.

This original definition of *charis* (grace) is what the Apostle Paul is re-establishing with the church at Ephesus in this passage. He was drawing from their daily social structures a picture of how the Kingdom of God operates. Their familiarity around the nature of grace is what excited the people in the region about the message Paul delivered. This familiarity and excitement is what is missing today about grace.

A HIGHER LEVEL OF GIVING

Where I'm about to take you now is into the heavenly realm of how the Kingdom of God views this matter. We have been looking at most of this reciprocal giving from the perspective of mankind's social interactions. Yet as we ascend into the heavenly places where we are seated with Jesus at the right hand of the throne of grace, we are going to begin to see an entirely different nature to the purpose of giving.

The first thing you will notice seated in the heavenly realm is that time truly is a line with a start and end, both of which you can see in the same moment. This is different from when you're in time since all you can see is what is directly in front of you (immediate future) or what is directly behind you (remembered history) – never both at once. The distance you are able to see in time is dictated by the significant events which you've established in either direction. In history it is a series of significant emotional events you are able to recall at will, while in the future it is a pre-determined goal that you are striving for.

From an eternal, kingdom perspective there is always the ability to see beyond the perspective of your sight in time, be it history or future. This makes possible a facet of grace's nature which I call *"forward giving,"* or the ability to give a gift in advance of when the gift is truly needed. Let me explain with an example: When I in my early twenties, one year for Christmas my grandfather gave me a gift which I felt was rather out of left field. He had gone to great lengths to assemble a package of items which would help in the event my car ever broke down. There was a hazard flashlight, flairs, emergency signs, and a whole assortment of devices which could be used to help in the event of a flat tire or mechanical emergency while on the road. The reason I felt this it was out of left field was because I didn't own a car at the time – I rode a bicycle! I recall at the time it was difficult to appreciate the benefit of such a gift yet I reluctantly accepted it and immediately put it in a box which subsequently sat in storage for a number of years.

After I was married, I retrieved the box from storage, and placed the contents in the trunk of my car which I now owned. About a month later, I was driving down the road and suddenly my tire blew out. When I got to the side of the road, I went to the trunk of my car and pulled out all of the equipment my grandfather had given to me so many years past. I was greatly appreciative of every item in that gift on the day I needed it.

The Kingdom of God has benefits set aside for each of us in a similar manner. The throne of grace sits over the line of time able to see in your life when you will need a benefit which can only come from a heavenly gift. This, the ability to give a gift in a forward nature, is expected of every person seated in heavenly places. You'll find mention of it in a number of scriptures yet for now the following one will be our highlight:

Bearing with one another, and forgiving one another, if anyone has a complaint against another; even as Christ forgave you, so you also must do. (14) But above all these things put on love, which is the bond of perfection. (Colossians 3:13-14)

Forward giving or *"forgiving"* as you'll find it in the scriptures is a function of grace. Both the word *"forgiving"* and *"forgave"* are grace words representing another facet of the nature of grace that has been lost. Notice in this passage as we act in a grace-manner we are representing the works of Christ from His throne of grace. Our ability to *"forward-give"* one another enables the recipient of our gift to overcome a difficulty in a future place. What they received from us will have perfected them, or made them whole, in love, so they can handle their moment with the grace of the kingdom. The reciprocal nature of grace will also insure you of a similar result in your future.

This is the high ground of grace which many are unaware of since forgiveness has such an emotional stronghold attached to it. However, to realize that the act of forgiveness is actually a gift from you so someone can overcome a future difficulty in their life places a new level of authority upon our actions which we've never possibly walked in. Yes, there may be pain, emotional or physical, attached to the matter, but you hold in your hands the opportunity to see to it that they succeed in a future mission which fulfills their destiny. Failure to forgive only delays success for them as well as for you.

Remember this: God, because of His great love for us, joyously gave a reciprocal grace-gift through His Son, Jesus, far in advance of when we would need it, so we could victoriously claim the overwhelming life that comes to us through His love for us.

> *The thief cometh not, but for to steal, and to kill, and to destroy: I am come that they might have life, and that they might have it more abundantly. (John 10:10)*

Jesus said the thief comes to steal, kill and destroy. It is three-pronged attack which the enemy will employ against every person on this planet. Have you had anything stolen from you? How about having something destroyed? I'll deal with the death issue in a moment. We've all had these things happen to us more than once in our lives. Many of you are still dealing with the bitter memories of these attacks and the impact they have had on your destiny. [9]

Jesus says He has come *"that they might have. . ."* This phrase is one Greek word in both of its occurrences here in this passage. It is the word *"echo"*, the same word we get the present day word *"echo."* Now you know what an echo is, don't you? Yep, a <u>reciprocal</u> sound effect. The unique property of an echo is that it replicates an original – it doesn't do anything different on its own accord. Also, an echo will dissipate over a period of time, but Jesus said it will *"more abound,"* which in the Greek means a violent, excessive, uncommon abundance. This means you are to have a life which expresses a previously spoken word and continue having an expression of that spoken word in a super-overwhelming fashion without end.

Recall that the joyous, grace-gift of God reciprocally given to you is a life like His. Jesus validates this claim stating He came to give us *"zōē"* life. Vine's Expository Dictionary defines this Greek word for life as:

---

[9] (What's interesting is that most insurance companies have an exclusion they call "Act of God" which protects them in the event of catastrophic events. They clearly don't know the difference between an act of God and that of the thief!)

Life as a principle, life in the absolute sense, life as God has it, that which the Father has in Himself, and which He gave to the Incarnate Son to have in Himself, and which the Son manifested in the world.

I've written about this in *Eternal Life. Yes, Forever!* But it bares repeating, briefly. The primary nature of the Kingdom of God is Life. There is no death anywhere in its realm. This life is eternal, everlasting. It goes on forever. There is not a single person who would deny this very aspect of the Kingdom of God. This is why so many desire to go to Heaven so they may have this life in them. Yet consider that Jesus came to give this life to you here on Earth, now. Yet so many find this truth...well...unbelievable. Our inability to accept a truth does not change its nature – it only changes our direction away from that truth. Consider this quote from Jesus:

> *"...making the word of God of no effect through your tradition which you have handed down. And many such things you do." (Mark 7:13)*

If you've read the Genesis account of the fall of man, you know how God said that in the day Adam ate the fruit from the tree of the knowledge of good and evil he would die. Well Adam ate it and he didn't die that day – at least not in the sense which we know of it. It took over 900 years for the first man to learn how to die. And we have so perfected this knowledge to a point where it only now takes most people 60 to 70 years to accomplish the same results. Our handed down tradition of death is more accepted to society - believers and unbelievers alike – than the word of God which believers even profess.

"But they died!" is what I'm hearing from you. I'm not being callous or heartless here. I too have experienced the pain that comes from death. So let's take a moment to consider this: Do you believe they

are in Heaven, in the Kingdom of God? Do you agree there is no death in that realm? Their earth suit may have retired but their spirit certainly didn't. They presently reside in a realm of such abounding grace, they wish you knew about it. There is an entire host in Heaven who is cheering over what you are now reading. They want all of us to finally embrace this truth and begin to live it out here on the Earth. Okay, let's get back to this matter of abundance.

If man had not sinned in the Garden of Eden, would he have died? If Jesus had not given His life, would He still be here today? These are not trick questions. They are foundational questions in understanding how grace operates because they both address the abundant nature of an eternal life.

> *Moreover the law entered, that the offense might abound. But where sin abounded, grace did much more abound: (21) That as sin hath reigned unto death, even so might grace reign through righteousness unto eternal life by Jesus Christ our Lord. (Romans 5:20-21)*

This passage in Romans 5 is a whole grace study in itself which, if time permits, I'll get to later, but for now, I want to focus on this point: Why does grace abound more than sin? Consider this: Some scientists say that today, the entire population of this planet exceeds all of the people who have ever lived on the planet previously. Life abounds more than death. I don't know if you realize this but death, and anything which resembles or leads to it, doesn't have a way of reproducing itself like life does. Life has the ability to create something called *"generations"* which echo the original pattern. Death is a one-trick pony while life is an entire circus.

Why does grace abound? It honors life. How did I arrive at this conclusion? Grace reigns through righteousness unto eternal life. *"Reign"* is a word which indicates a position of supreme authority and the entire honor the position represents. *"Righteousness"* means right-standing, correct, according to right thinking. So let's assemble this together from verse 21: From the environment of an eternal, everlasting life joyous, reciprocal giving correctly operates from a governing preeminence far beyond the affect of what sin can produce. This life abounding nature of grace is what you have been saved into; this is your heritage, and how you express it on Earth is your destiny in Christ Jesus.

Are you beginning to see the importance of grace from the perspective of the King? Then why have we allowed ourselves to live as paupers on Earth when it is not the intent of the King? Whose echo are you resounding?

THE BELIEVING OF GRACE

We all know that the transaction of giving involves two or more parties and there is an object which transfers from one party to the other party (parties) in the transaction. One has an object that provides a benefit to the other upon its release. Pretty standard stuff that you're not going to get all worked up about, right? What I mean by worked up is that you're not the least bit excited right now; you're not clinging on with anticipation; you're not feeling adrenaline surge through your body with a heightened sense of awareness; you know, *"worked up."* Why not?

As you read this material have you recognized the exchange? Is there something you receive in these writings you're not receiving elsewhere? Is it possible we have become so accustomed to *"taking"* that we have lost our ability to recognize the act of giving?

Before you go and think I'm looking for affirmation here (I'm not) you should consider that our social structure today has conditioned us to *"take."* We live in a limit-minded society so you had better take what is given to you because you don't know when, or even if, there will be any more. It is feast or famine out there so you better get while the getting is good! Get what you can, can what you get and then sit on the can. Do unto others before they do it to you. Get the point? We are accustomed to taking.

We are accustomed to taking for one reason: we believe and we trust in scarcity. We even have a faith for scarcity.

Have you ever been to a buffet restaurant? There is placed before you generous amounts of food in such variety that it sometime boggles the mind. If you watch the people who dine in these places you'll see the effect of scarcity thinking. Surrounded by unlimited resources they pile their plates high before *"it's all gone."* Furthermore, they'll watch from their table their favorite dish in the distance just so they can make sure they get another serving before it runs out. It's a buffet – food doesn't run out!

The Kingdom of God is like a buffet restaurant – abounding grace and provision. We can't grasp this. Scarcity has mothered us and we can't pull ourselves off of the teat because we believe we'll starve. It's the <u>only thing</u> keeping us going right now. One of the names of God is *El Shaddai*, the many breasted one. This name speaks of abundant provision beyond compare. But we have limited our belief to *"there will always be feast and famine."* Never do we consider the perspective of the kingdom – feast, the famine has been consumed! Consider this verse:

> *For God so loved the world, that he gave his only begotten Son, that whosoever believeth in him should not perish, but have everlasting life. (John 3:16)*

Do you see any scarcity in this verse? It is there as a condition of one thing: believing. The question to answer is do you believe because of the scarcity in your life or because of the abundance in the kingdom? How you believe determines how you interact with all of the facets of grace. Did you believe because of the lack found in perishing or in the abundance of a life everlasting? Before you answer this question realize that you can't answer it correctly, simply because neither - the lack nor the abundance - is what you are to believe in. Yet these are what so many believers place their focus upon – the affect of grace.

Let me pause here for a moment to deal with a matter of grammatical usage of two words: affect and effect. Webster's states it this way: Affect implies the action of a stimulus which can produce a response or reaction; effect goes beyond mere influence, it refers to actual achievement of a final result. Keep these definitions in mind because grace is both!

In the kingdom of grace the one thing you focus on, or believe in, is the gift – not the affect that happens from receiving the gift. The gift creates the affect, life to those who trust it, death to those who reject it. To operate in the kingdom of grace you have to believe in the gift in order to give it to others out of a reciprocal nature. You have to believe the gift will address every issue where scarcity exists. You have to believe the gift doesn't need to be added to or subtracted from in order to fulfill its purpose. You have to believe the gift answers all hopes and is the evidence to all its effects.

Do you believe in the transaction of grace to this degree? If you find it hard to do so, then you may want to take the admonishment of Jesus and come to the kingdom as a little child. Children don't believe from a place of scarcity which means they don't focus on affects. Have you ever watched a small child open gifts either at a birthday or Christmas time? The focus of every child during one of these events is on the gift – singular – while every other gift waits to be unwrapped.

When one gift is unwrapped the child will naturally play with that gift ignoring the other gifts around them for a time.

This is how we are to operate with the gift from the Kingdom that we receive. There is an abundance of other gifts for us to receive, but our focus is to be pin-pointed on just this one gift – Jesus. From Him all other gifts come, each abounding with the joyous, eternal life-giving, reciprocal nature of grace.

So with this understanding of the role of believing in grace, you are now ready to see how the gift of grace can be used in the manner the Kingdom expects it to be used in.

Activating Grace

You've probably all seen it: A large family gathering around a meal. Adults, and children alike, jockey for positions next to their favorite foodstuffs which surround the tablescape. Everyone is chattering about the vast array before them and the hunger they each are so overpowered by. The matron of the house generally will survey the flock before her and with a sweeping gesture of grabbing the hand of those on each side of her, draw the attention to all those attending that a solemn moment is about to be administered which will require silence from all. Following some unwritten protocol she will ask the head of the household to say *"grace."*

As a child I was tortured by the *"saying of grace"* before a meal. It was merely another means for adults to dictate how they felt I should behave in a social setting. It prolonged a ravenous appetite which would better be served by just letting me indulge in the delicacies set before me. There was no purpose served by this ritualistic delay of game tactic. The delay only gave me time to devise my offensive assault on the food to get my servings before my brother, which resulted in much clamor and arguing after the moment of silence. So let me ask this most basic of question to our traditions: Should we see something happen when we say *"grace?"*

There is a whole world that opens to you once you understand the purpose and significance of *"saying grace"* and the key it plays in the Kingdom of God. So let's look at it properly. Many know that *"saying* grace" is offering a prayer at the meal. But why is it called *"grace"* and not prayer? The Disciples Prayer[10] does give us some clues.

> *After this manner therefore pray ye: Our Father which art in heaven, Hallowed be thy name. (10) Thy kingdom come. Thy will be done in earth, as it is in heaven. (11) Give us this day our daily bread. (12) And forgive us our debts, as we forgive our debtors. (13) And lead us not into temptation, but deliver us from evil: For thine is the kingdom, and the power, and the glory, for ever. Amen. (Matthew 6:9-13)*

So where do you think the clue is? It's obvious, right? No, it's not, *"Give us this day our daily bread."* If you thought it was, don't feel bad – many think so. The clue is the line just prior to that. *"Your kingdom come. Your will be done..."* is the clue. Recall that this study in grace is based from the perspective of the Kingdom of God. So any prayer we are going to talk about, particularly one which has to do with a meal, we had better understand it from His realm rather than from the realm of our needs. After all, our entire preparation here on earth is to get us ready for the marriage supper of the Lamb!

KINGDOM PRAYERS

There are a number of locations about the globe which are recognized as prayer centers connected to Heaven. In these places there reside a number of people who are gifted in teaching on the various types of prayers found in the Bible. In these places the Kingdom prayer is essential to seeing God move on the Earth.

A Kingdom prayer is one which opens a portal so that His Kingdom comes on Earth just as it is in Heaven. This means we'll experience the

---

[10] Many call it the Lord's Prayer until the realization that the disciples asked Him to model for them how they should pray to the Father.

fullness of the realm of grace on Earth. These prayers are not based on formulas more than on a relationship with the Father just as Jesus had. A prayer which is based on relationship doesn't feature needs.

Recollect for a moment the last three prayer times or prayer meetings you've experienced. How much time was spent on earthly needs? Finances, health, personal relationships, lost loved ones, and so many other needs interrupt our time learning how to relate to the Father. Consider for a moment that Adam prior to the fall lived from the Kingdom of grace on Earth. In this place he was able to distinguish when the Father would come into the garden in the cool of the day. The fall interrupted his ability to learn how to relate with the Father and shifted his focus onto the mercy of the Father to fulfill his needs.

Jesus, the last Adam, had thirty years to develop and perfect how to operate from the realm of grace. Jesus told us He only did those things He saw the Father doing. That type of insight can only come from a relationship which is focused solely on the Father. The last three and half years of His earthly ministry depict how grace is to operate on Earth as it is in Heaven. Not once do we see Jesus wringing His hands over a need – even the most pressing need.

ATTITUDE GAINS ALTITUDE

Our mission is to bring the environment which permeates from the throne of grace into a situation through a prayer. I assure you when this occurs, every need will be overwhelmed by the abounding nature of grace. Yet it all begins with your attitude. This is not rocket science here: If you're seeking for grace, what attitude do you suppose should be evident? If you said *"grateful,"* congratulations! Being grateful is a display of grace! This is the primary attitude which accesses the throne of God. It acknowledges His superior nature to deal favorably for you in every circumstance. It re-positions God over a problem that has tried to overwhelm our sights. Remember that grace is an altitude as well as an attitude.

"But I am grateful when I pray," is what I'm hearing, *"and nothing is happening."* Let me say two things here. 1.) *"Nothing"* is impossible with God. So the second part of your statement now reads, *"and impossible is happening."* Your lack of faith in your own prayer will still move God to do something if for no other reason then to shake you out of your stupor. 2.) Gratefulness has a language that is easy to identify. If you're not speaking it then how do I, let alone God, know you're grateful? Don't pull that *"God knows what's in my heart,"* bit either. The Bible says out of the abundance of the heart the mouth speaks. If you're grateful – meaning full of grace – you'll speak the language and everyone will recognize it. So what is the language of someone full of grace? Let's go look at the Master.

THE PRAYER THAT ABOUNDS

I recently heard a teaching from a very well known man of God, one who I've followed for a number of years. His teaching had to do with our words and prayers aligning with what the Bible clearly declares.

In his message, he kept referring to the things we do which aren't even written in the Bible, but we act as though they are. One example he gave caught me completely off guard. He said, *"Show me where it says in the Bible that we're supposed to say grace before a meal. There is not one place where that is found!"*

What caught me was that I knew differently, and it became a moment in my study on grace that validated all I had learned. Yes, technically, the command is not found in the Bible; however the example is very much present. Furthermore, the word *"grace"* is not the interpretive word which is used in the example. So let's go look at this because you might be surprised at what that interpretive word is.

There is only one story about Jesus which appears in each of the four gospels. It is the story of Jesus feeding the multitude. Most of us have heard of this story more times than we may want to recall (especially if you grew up in the church!) This time I want you to suspend any other rendition you've heard about this matter and look at it now from the perspective of grace operating from the Kingdom of God. Furthermore, I want to nip in the bud the lame excuse that this happened because of the deity of Jesus. I hope to one day exorcise this rotten religious spirit from you, but for now understand that in this example (plus every other one up until his resurrection) Jesus was operating as a man upon Earth. Any claim he has as a deity does not exist on this world until his resurrection.

We know the party line about this story: Jesus and his disciples are out on the road preaching for three days and everybody is hanging on His every word. So enthralled are they that they even refuse to eat. The disciples are concerned they will have to deal with people dying on them in the wilderness so they ask Jesus to disperse the crowd into the surrounding communities to find something to eat. To their dismay Jesus tells the disciples to feed the people. A quick inventory of their resources unveils a lunch from a child consisting of five barley loaves and two fish. Jesus instructs the disciples to make the people sit down as he prepares to feed the people.

Five barley loaves and two fish. Five thousand men, plus women and children. Feed them.

Do you see any need here? You're a disciple right? Is there a need? First rule of discipleship: *"Your kingdom come, your will be done on earth as in heaven. Give us..."* What is the main attribute of grace? Reciprocal giving. What is Jesus planning to feed them with?

Something a little child **gave** him. What happens next is vital to understanding this whole topic and securing your access to the throne of grace. I'm going to give you the sequence from each gospel so you can see it yourself.

> Then He commanded the multitudes to sit down on the grass. And He took the five loaves and the two fish, and looking up to heaven, He blessed and broke and gave the loaves to the disciples; and the disciples gave to the multitudes. (Matthew 14:19)

> And when He had taken the five loaves and the two fish, He looked up to heaven, blessed and broke the loaves, and gave them to His disciples to set before them; and the two fish He divided among them all. (Mark 6:41)

> Then He took the five loaves and the two fish, and looking up to heaven, He blessed and broke them, and gave them to the disciples to set before the multitude. (Luke 9:16)

> And Jesus took the loaves, and when He had given thanks He distributed them to the disciples, and the disciples to those sitting down; and likewise of the fish, as much as they wanted (John 6:11)

Alright, what is the difference? I don't want what is the same, but what is different. In this example, it is the difference which is the rule (I'll explain that in a moment). Did you find it? Okay, look at the verse from John 6. Notice in this rendition of the story John states that Jesus gave thanks for the loaves and the fish, while in each of the other versions it says Jesus blessed the loaves and fish. So what is the big deal here – three to bless, one to thank? Any of you who have been around sound biblical teaching know how every scripture must be confirmed by at least two or more witnesses in order to be valid, right? Three to one is pretty clear, right? John 6 is an anomaly, right? Consider this verse:

> *however, other boats came from Tiberias, near the place where they ate bread after the Lord had given thanks. (John 6:23)*

This is right after the feeding of the multitude and the disciple are sent across the lake and Jesus walks across the water to meet them. This particular verse describes the place where the multitude had been fed by giving reference to the thanks which occurred.

What? This doesn't fit the test case because it's the same author just describing the previous event. Okay. I guess in order for this to fit the rule I'll have to pull out all the stops. You do know that Jesus did this same miracle more than once, don't you? Yep, he also feed four thousand men plus woman and children. Notice their occurrence.

> *And He took the seven loaves and the fish and gave thanks, broke them and gave them to His disciples; and the disciples gave to the multitude. (Matthew 15:36)*

> *So He commanded the multitude to sit down on the ground. And He took the seven loaves and gave thanks, broke them and gave them to His disciples to set before them; and they set them before the multitude. (Mark 8:6)*

I believe from these two entries, according to the rules of verse verification, the score now stands at (3) bless to (3) thank. A tie! Big deal, right? (Don't you just hate petty competitions about defining the meaning of Bible verses?) Let's step back for a moment and look at the purpose of why we're traveling down this path.

If you'll recall, I am trying to show you what the language of gratitude is from Jesus. My claim is Jesus never had a need that He expressed to the Father even when faced with the daunting task of feeding the multitude – twice! The language He expressed in each of these occurrences activated the throne of grace in a time of need, not out of mercy - as an expression of suspended judgment - more rather like *chesed* - as equals sharing consideration and kindliness - but from the very nature of abounding grace. The key component of the language of gratitude is the word transcribed as "thanks." In Greek it is *eucharisteō*. According to Strong's Concordance the meaning of this word is: *to be grateful, to express gratitude, **to say grace at a meal;** give thanks.*

Did you catch that? Saying grace means giving thanks at a meal. *"Whew! Boy that was the longest teaching on thanks I ever read. Big deal! I'll try to remember this next time I'm chosen to say grace at mom's house."*

NOW THE REST OF THE STORY.

If you trace the root meaning of the word *eucharisteō* you will soon discover that *charis*, or grace, is contained within it. The prefix of *"eu"* has the meaning of good, which would render this word as *"good grace."* We already have seen that it is the Father's *good* pleasure to give us the kingdom. So it appears that *"thanks"* has a substantial role in activating grace into a *"need"*. But I want to draw your attention to something out of the passage from Mark 8 so you can see this miracle in a whole new light.

> *So He commanded the multitude to sit down on the ground. And He took the seven loaves and gave thanks, broke them and gave them to His disciples to set before them; and they set them before the multitude. (7) They also had a few small fish; and having blessed them, He said to set them also before them (Mark 8:6-7)*

A kingdom prayer has the ability to activate the abounding nature of grace into an earthly need and overwhelm it as well as activate the original intent and nature of a thing to fulfill its purpose. In this passage from Mark we see how Jesus gives thanks for the bread. This activates grace to begin its abounding nature. But this also has deeper significance. Jesus, acting in a priestly role here is offering thanks for this bread. Recall, Jesus says in the book of John that He is the bread of life. This bread is representing His own body, a point which He will fully disclose to the disciples at the last supper.

Yet even before this, Jesus is referencing what would be known in the book of Leviticus as the thank offering. This is a very unique offering for the people of Israel since it was the only bread offering which permitted leaven to be used in its composition; and it was the offering meant to be shared by the people and the priests at the time it was given. We see in this one reference Jesus traveling through many venues toward fulfilling this need of the crowd.

Notice in the second aspect of this verse that the fish were not thanked for but were blessed. The reason for this has to do with recognizing Kingdom purpose. When a purpose is clearly defined, grace is not able to add to it – it simply activates it. When the fish were created in the Genesis account, God clearly ". . . *blessed them and said 'be fruitful and multiply.'*" Jesus, operating from the Kingdom of grace, simply reminded the fish of their original purpose and they began to multiply.

So in summary here, Jesus reviews the materials He has to work with in the situation and seeing the loaves of bread, He offers thanks, or says *"grace"* for them, to the Father; hands them over to the disciples to be dispersed, who witness the abounding nature of grace in their hands as they release a gift given from a child into the hands of all who ask. Furthermore, Jesus reminds the fish of their original purpose and they too multiply from the hands of the disciples. At the end, in each occurrence, baskets are filled with the fragments attesting to the abounding nature of the Kingdom of grace in its operation.

Let me ask you the same question I asked at the opening: Should we see something happen when we say *"grace?"* If we understand the nature of grace, I would say the next time your asked to say grace, you better see first if there is a Kingdom purpose not being fulfilled which needs to be activated by way of a blessing, then ask yourself if everyone is ready to eat the abundance which grace will produce from your thanks.

THE WILL OF GRACE

Yes, grace has a purpose, a desire, a pleasure associated with it that you must understand simply because it is the motivation of its operation – an operation which has been on-going even before the foundation of this world was laid. So let's take a look at this matter – again from the perspective of the Kingdom of God.

> *Your kingdom come. Your will be done On earth as it is in heaven. (Matthew 6:10)*

> *But seek first the kingdom of God and His righteousness, and all these things shall be added to you. (Matthew 6:33)*

> *"Do not fear, little flock, for it is your Father's good pleasure to give you the kingdom. (Luke 12:32)*

Each of these verses informs us about the Kingdom of God's intent in our lives. The first shows us that the Kingdom is to be represented and performing on Earth; the second shows us that we are the ones who are to bring this representation to earth; and the third clearly establishes that the Father wants to give the Kingdom to us.

Even the most cursory glance at these scriptures will bring to light that the word *"grace"* does not appear within them, so how can I possibly use them in talking about grace? Obviously, they each mention the Kingdom; and a kingdom is defined as the domain or territory a king possesses and rules over; and the king rules from a throne, which in this matter at hand has been described in the book of Hebrews as the *"throne of grace."* So understand that any time you come across the phrase *"Kingdom of God"* or *"Kingdom of Heaven,"* grace – embodied in a throne of rule and authority – is present and operating. There is no possible way for one to exist without the other.

This places a whole new dynamic on these verses if you include the element of grace in them. Matthew 6:10 would then read, *"Your Kingdom of grace come. Your will be done on earth as it is in heaven."* Matthew 6:33 would read, *"But seek first the Kingdom of God's grace and His righteousness, and all these things shall be added to you."* And Luke 12:32 would clearly show all the attributes of grace we've uncovered so far with, *"Do not fear, little flock, for it is your Father's good pleasure to give you the Kingdom of grace."* This is a completely different way of thinking about the actions of grace in our lives. It may startle many that grace is so inclusive in the Kingdom, yet it has always been this way. The traditional teachings we've had about grace, and even the Kingdom, while good in their purpose, were not complete in their understanding. And I'll be the first to admit that even this teaching is still being unfolded to me.

So keeping this new perspective of the relationship of grace and the Kingdom in mind, what then is the will of grace? Matthew 6:10 alludes to it, *". . .your will be done. . ."* and as I stated *"will"* represents a purpose, a desire, a pleasure, so we see again this being alluded to in Luke 12:32, *". . .good pleasure..."* Yet is there a clearly defined *"will"* of the Kingdom for us? Yes, there are a number of passages which state what is the will of the Kingdom is for us. I'm going to focus on a single passage at this time which clearly defines the Kingdom of grace.

Rejoice always, pray without ceasing, in everything give thanks; for this is the will of God in Christ Jesus for you. (1 Thessalonians 5:16-18)

Rejoice, pray, give thanks. This is the will of grace. I know it says this is the will of God, but I want you to see grace here as it truly exists. In this passage the two words that I want to draw your attention to are *"rejoice"* and *"thanks"* which are *"grace words"* found in Strong's Concordance as G5463 and G2168 respectively. Both of these actions are *"grace-events"* in the Kingdom. Rejoice, *chairo* in Greek, is the root word for the definition of grace; thanks, *eucharisteō* in Greek, was the topic I covered in addressing our attitude of thankfulness. Notice how your unceasing prayers are bracketed between two *"grace-events"*, or put another way, your prayers are covered by grace, so long as you do the first and the last also. These three actions represent the will of the Father in His greatest grace-gift, Christ Jesus.

I have known many people who never really knew what the will of the Father was for their life even though they dutifully prayed the disciple's prayer from Matthew 6. I think much of the difficulty they've had is, from a Kingdom perspective, understanding **they don't have a life.** Any life they want to claim they have in the Kingdom is only through Christ Jesus and that life operates in the nature of grace. All activities in this Kingdom life spring from the will, purpose, desire or pleasure of the Father. All He asks of us is to rejoice, pray, and give thanks. It's pretty simple, right? Then why do we try to do everything else but this? It is possible we don't understand how to... Oh, that is for a different book to cover. Until then, I will rejoice, pray, and give thanks for you.

Grace is not...

I'm going to slay a religious cow.

In this journey through the understanding of grace, I have tried to show you that the nature of grace is multi-faceted – one aspect cannot properly define it completely. I have repeatedly stated that my perspective was from the Kingdom of God; meaning I was not going to limit these writings to how grace affects us in time, but how grace operates in the eternal realm. There is a slight difficulty to this in that our language is reflective of time and not eternity, yet the text we refer to is 2,000 years old and older. This is the paradox we confront. Furthermore, since we are not familiar with the customs and practices of the times when the text was written, we try to attach present-day meanings to topics and occurrences which appear "un-natural" to us. So now I'm going to attack a present day mindset which limits our ability to access the nature of grace. I trust that when I'm through the renewing of your mind will enable you to move into an elevated state of Kingdom thinking. Prepare yourself for a journey.

UNMERITED FAVOR

Ask any pastor or biblical teacher to define grace and they will most commonly respond, *"The unmerited favor of God."* You have throughout these writings probably been harboring this definition in the back of your mind as an anchor to what you know grace to be. So why call it into question now? Because I believe that the term was forged by a sin consciousness in order to control your behavior.

Is it possible since you know a bit more now about grace that there may have been some deception set afoot which kept you blinded to the possibilities grace truly holds? The only way to determine this is to look at how the definition was arrived at and then determine if it is accurate enough to be the singular, all-encompassing definition for grace. So let's take a look at how these two words are defined in order to bring them together in our text.

According to any good dictionary you'll find the term *"unmerited"* defined as, *"Not earned or deserved."* Favor will have a more complex meaning depending on its use.

noun	1. A gracious, friendly, or obliging act that is freely granted: do someone a favor.
	Friendly or favorable regard; approval or support: won the favor of the monarch; looked with favor on the plan.
	A state of being held in such regard: a style currently in favor.
	2. Unfair partiality; favoritism.
	A privilege or concession.
	favors Sexual privileges, especially as granted by a woman.
	3. Something given as a token of love, affection, or remembrance.
	A small decorative gift given to each guest at a party.
	4. Advantage; benefit: sailed under favor of cloudless skies.
	5. Behalf; interest: an error in our favor.
	6. Obsolete. A communication, especially a letter.
	7. Archaic.

	Aspect or appearance.	
	Countenance; face.	
verb	1.	To perform a kindness or service for; oblige.
	2.	To treat or regard with friendship, approval, or support.
	3.	To be partial to; indulge a liking for: favors bright colors.
	4.	To be or tend to be in support of.
	5.	To make easier or more possible; facilitate: Darkness favored their escape.
	6.	To treat with care; be gentle with: favored my wounded leg.

I think from the information we've gotten within these two words we can accurately describe *"unmerited favor"* as an unearned friendly act of favoritism given as a support or service. Is there anything about this definition which strikes you as odd? If not, then please carefully read it again because this is where we are going to go next.

JESUS, OUR PATTERN

> *And the child grew, and waxed strong in spirit, filled with wisdom: and the grace of God was upon him. (Luke 2:40)*

> *And the Word was made flesh, and dwelt among us, (and we beheld his glory, the glory as of the only begotten of the Father,) full of grace and truth. (John 1:14)*

In both of these passages both Luke and John open their gospel with a description of Jesus which includes how grace was operating through him. If you, like me, have read these passages enough, you don't really stop to consider what these two writers are trying to say here. You just take the term *"grace"* at face value, or should I say at a value which doesn't require thinking. But let's consider this word *"grace"* now with the definition that we have from above and see if this sounds correct.

> And the child grew, and waxed strong in spirit, filled with wisdom: and [the unearned friendly act of favoritism given as a support or service of God] was upon him. (Luke 2:40 revised)

> And the Word was made flesh, and dwelt among us, (and we beheld his glory, the glory as of the only begotten of the Father,) full of [the unearned friendly act of favoritism given as a support or service] and truth. (John 1:14 revised)

Is it just me or does this somehow not *"flow"* the way it should? Maybe it's just the verse selection that doesn't work here; after all, grace does mean *"unmerited favor."* Fair enough, let's try these two verses also from Luke and John.

> And Jesus increased in wisdom and stature, and in favor with God and man. (Luke 2:52)

> And of his fulness have all we received, and grace for grace. (John 1:16)

Whoa! In the first verse, the word *"favor"* is the same word in the Greek we call "grace." So shouldn't this really read, *"And Jesus increased in wisdom and stature, and in <u>unmerited favor</u> with God and* *man,"* while the second verse should read, *"And of his fulness have all we received, and <u>unmerited favor</u> for <u>unmerited favor</u>."* In the words of the famous poet-statesmen Bugs Bunny, *"What's up, doc?"*

THE SET UP

Okay, I admit that I set you up selecting these four verses. Notice how I didn't have to go very far in either of these writer's gospels to find the use of grace. Yet, I also want you to understand how the *"pat"* definition of grace will not work for every occurrence of the word *"grace"* which we come across in our reading. If I can do this with just four verses, what do you think that someone controlled by a religious spirit can do within an entire doctrine? This is why I'm taking a defining approach with the topic of grace. I can safely say we've been set up, again. The question is, *"How?"*

THE CAUSE

To understand this, we need to go back in time to when the Apostle Paul was in the city of Ephesus. Situated in the south-western region of present day Turkey, Ephesus was the second largest city in both population and political importance in all of the Roman Empire. Historians believe the Apostle John wrote his gospel while residing in Ephesus and this also established its position in the Book of Revelations which he wrote some years later.

Its prominence in the region had been established even before the reign of Alexander the Great. This was a thriving commercial metropolis which had been, and continued to be, at the crossroads to empires. Acts 19 describes Paul's entry into the city and his subsequent two year daily teaching ministry which he conducted in the city. I believe that the church in this community was the apple of Paul's eye considering the manner in which he departed from them in Acts 20. Years later, while confined in a prison in Rome, Paul would write a letter to this church which some theologians call *"the grandest glimpse into the heart of the Father."* Contained within its opening passage is the longest sentence in the entire New Testament. Comprising eleven verses, it clearly establishes the plan and purpose of the Father before the foundation of the world. Yet it is in the second chapter of this letter where our definition of *"unmerited favor"* is realized in the following verses.

> *And hath raised us up together, and made us sit together in heavenly places in Christ Jesus: (7) That in the ages to come he might shew the exceeding riches of his grace in his kindness toward us through Christ Jesus. (8) For by grace are ye saved through faith; and that not of yourselves: it is the gift of God: (9) Not of works, lest any man should boast. (10) For we are his workmanship, created in Christ Jesus unto good works, which God hath before ordained that we should walk in them. (Ephesians 2:6-10)*

Verse 8 established the truth that grace is a gift as I wrote about previously. This sentence covers the *"favor"* definition we established above. The aspect of verse 9 is what defines the *"unmerited"* clause of the grace definition. If you, as many do, stop here, the definition of unmerited favor is correct and acceptable for almost every occurrence of the word grace. But is it correct in context, both scripturally and historically? I would have to say...

SITTING NEXT TO WHAT?

There is a deeper explanation to verse 9 that needs to be brought out here. In verse 6, *"...made us sit together in heavenly places in Christ Jesus:"* which establishes our position in God's Kingdom, a position that is shared with, and in, Christ. We are told in the book of Hebrews how Jesus sits at the right hand of the Father, which means that if He does, so do we. So for a moment, I want you to visualize that you're sitting there, at the right hand of the Father. I want you to get a feel for how the seat feels on your skin; what it's like to hold onto the arms of the chair; to lean back into it. Take your time – there is no rush, after all you belong there. Okay now take your left hand and reach out to touch the chair beside you. Go ahead, touch it. What did you just touch? That's right, the Father's throne – the throne of grace. Your Father just let you touch His throne. My question to you is this: Was this *"unmerited favor"* you just experienced? Before you answer that, consider this.

In a kingdom, the only people who are permitted to be on the same elevation as the king are family members. In the example above you didn't have to reach up to the throne but across to the throne. Ephesians 1 tells us about how we became sons in this Kingdom.

> *Blessed be the God and Father of our Lord Jesus Christ, who hath blessed us with every spiritual blessing in the heavenly places in Christ: (4) even as he chose us in him before the foundation of the world, that we should be holy and without blemish before him in love: (5) having foreordained us unto adoption as sons through Jesus Christ unto himself, according to the good pleasure of his will, (Ephesians 1:3-5)*

Before time, before Earth, you and I were chosen in Christ Jesus for adoption as sons.[11] Now this is vitally important to understand here because the word for *"son"* which Paul uses here has special significance and relates solely to our discussion from the passage out of Ephesians 2. In the Greek there are two words for *"son."* One, which the Apostle John uses in his writings, describes a son who is born into the family; while the *"son"* that the Apostle Paul uses in his writings is for a son who is a legal heir to the family. The difference is

---

[11] I address more about this in the chapter "The Sons of Grace."

that a legal heir has vested powers to act on behalf of the head of the family in every matter. This authority was often signified in public through an adoption ceremony. You can always be part of the family as a son, but you can only act as the father would act if society recognizes you're adopted. So how does this apply to our scriptures?

Paul is describing to the Ephesians how the Kingdom of God differs from the kingdoms of this world. In the first chapter of Ephesians he clearly defines the pattern of the Kingdom of God. By the time he reaches the second chapter, Paul now is showing the differences between the two. In verse 6, Paul positions us in heavenly places next to the throne, yet verse 9, he explains the difference of how we arrived there versus the manner by which all of Ephesus' society operated under.

In the Roman and Greek societies of the day when Paul was writing these words, it was quite common to *"work"* for positions of power either through servitude or by buying favors from a benefactor. The Roman ruling classes often adopted sons from other families in order to maintain an heir to their position. These arrangements were fully recognized within the social order of the day, and were quite common in large cities like Rome and Ephesus where the ability to rule depended on strong alliances across many family lines.

What Paul is putting forth here in the second chapter is that position within God Kingdom cannot be bought or sold nor can you obtain it through any other manipulation of family structures. God had already predetermined what the protocol would be for entrance: It would be a gift of priceless value which for ages to come people would recognize.

If ye then, being evil, know how to give good gifts unto your children, how much more shall your Father which

is in heaven give good things to them that ask him?
(Matthew 7:11)

CAN "UNMERITED" BE ASSOCIATED WITH "FAVOR"?

So let's wrap up this matter of *"unmerited favor."* Is it warranted as a definition of grace? Let me ask you a few questions first. If you give your child a gift, is it unmerited? If you give your spouse a gift, is it unmerited? If your parents ever gave you a gift, was it unmerited? I believe the answer to each of these questions relies on the relationship you have with the person. Personally speaking, I can say that every one of those questions can be answered with, *"no it was merited."* My kids and spouse deserved every gift I gave them because of the love I have for them, and I believe my parents felt the same way towards me. Yes, there may have been times where I tried to work for a gift, or had one of my children do the same thing to me. But the result was never what was expected. I think we have allowed these two words be joined together in an unholy alliance seeped in the effects of a sin consciousness. They make about as much sense as the term *"jumbo shrimp"* or *"long-haired bald man."*

Our Father's plan and purpose has been established in eternity past and He hasn't changed it. If Jesus found favor with Him and man, then we have the same nature available to us too. But if we keep attaching *"unmerited"* to it then no wonder we aren't doing the greater works Jesus said that we should do. Even Paul says in Ephesians 2:10 that we've been pre-ordained to do those works, but if you believe that the grace you operate in is unmerited, or not deserving, this is what you will get. This is leading me to...

Frustrating Grace

> *I do not frustrate the grace of God: for if righteousness come by the law, then Christ is dead in vain. (Galatians 2:21)*

The book of Galatians is Paul's address to a body of believers who had been swayed by the religious spirit in a band of traveling Jewish practitioners who claimed the need to perform the rituals of the Law as a means to practicing their faith in God and the works of Jesus. In this book Paul lays out a very concise argument for faith in the work of Christ, yet in doing so he draws attention to this concept of frustrating grace. This is the foremost problem a believer has to confront in their life as they move into the Kingdom mentality. Religious spirits utilize this as a tool to control a believer which I'll demonstrate in moment.

What Is So Frustrating?

We all know what frustration is and have at one time or another been hampered by it, so I don't need to define it for you. I decided to look at how the various translators used this word in this passage. Terms such as make void, set aside, repudiate, and nullify are all being used to describe *"frustrate."* Obviously with terms such as these, it might be better to understand what could possibly be behind this *"frustration."*Let me explain it with a very simple and oh-so-common experience.

Have you ever presented a gift to someone who you cared about, a gift you spent either a significant amount of time finding, or money acquiring, only to hear this from them, *"Oh! You shouldn't have. I can't take this."* In this exchange, how often have you responded, *"Yes, I got it for you. Please take it,"* only to hear, *"No, I can't. It's too much."* In someone's life the process of this one exchange may have become very protracted and ended in a manner which was a complete opposite to what was originally intended. Guess what? This entire scenario is known as **frustrating grace**. But how is this possible?

> *Every good gift and every perfect gift is from above, and cometh down from the Father of lights, with whom is no variableness, neither shadow of turning. (James 1:17)*

When someone uses the term "every" what is left out? Not one thing, correct? So James tells us that a gift which is good and perfect in its nature (why wouldn't any gift have these characteristics) is all-inclusive in its scope too, and these types of gifts come from the Father. *"But what does this have to do with the necklace I tried to give to my daughter-in-law or the new car I tried to give to my son and his wife? I was the one giving it to them."* God uses us to promote the Kingdom in the lives of those around us and one of the methods He employs is giving of gifts. (This is what grace is about after all!)

THE CULPRIT

But what is behind these actions either by others or by our self towards others? Those who are influenced with a religious spirit will say that their humility keeps them from being overcome by the trappings of this world. I have to say this is very noble and a whole lot of lawn fertilizer from farm animals too! (You know what I mean.) The true name for this false sense of humility is called "pride." Before you get all puckered up here you better understand why I make this claim.

When we make the claim we can't take a gift for "X" reason, we have displayed our *"choke point"* or self-imposed limitation on what the Kingdom of God is able to place in our lives. Grace's nature is to give and do it abundantly, but God will not give beyond what you're capable of receiving. God already gave the greatest gift of all through His son Jesus and every gift is simply an extension leading us back to the gift. Remember, it is the goodness of God which leads all men to repentance and His goodness is ultimately displayed in His Son.

When we choke on a gift, we are saying in essence, *"No, I can't take this, Jesus didn't give enough for me; I'm the only one who can give what's required."* I realize this statement doesn't sound pretty (or smell pretty for that matter!) but pride, at its inner most core, acts this way. *"Well, I never..."* Please stop for a moment and consider this. Have you ever wondered why Jesus said we should approach the Kingdom like little children? **Have you ever seen a little child turn down a gift?** A child knows nothing of pride until they meet an adult who wants to control their actions.

Religious spirits act the same way and want to control your actions by helping the homeless, childless, orphaned, and pregnant, drug addicted convicts of the world as a means of showing your worthiness since obviously your tithes and offerings are not moving God to work on your behalf. Even the mere tokens (gifts) which you get are placed before you to lure you into unholy acceptance on the things of this world, which we all know will perish in the end anyway, and keep you from... Do I need to go on here?

THE RULE OF THE KINGDOM OF GRACE

Gifts in all of their variety of forms come from the Father. They have been preordained to aid you in the works which have been prepared for you long before the foundation of this world was even laid. These gifts point you to the goodness of your Father and no matter how it is delivered to you its sole purpose is to cause you to offer abundant thanks to the Father for His great love for you. When any gift is presented to you, the rule of the Kingdom of Grace is simple: Always gratefully take the gift. In doing so, you keep the abounding environment of grace functioning in your life.

Remember: Always gratefully take the gift.

PART II - LITTLE GRACE!

"Can you give me a little grace here?"

Knowing what you now understand about grace, is it possible to comply with this request? Since grace is an abounding action, can a *"little"* be given? What really is being asked in this statement?

Consider how before this study your thoughts about being saved by grace were based upon the sin consciousness which permeated your thinking. Grace, in this capacity, was your life-line from being cast into the lake of fire. While this probably is still true, grace does so much more.

A sin conscious person always views grace as a life line, or crutch, to get them beyond the *"fallen"* nature they demonstrate. Whether they realize it or not, they have decided to stay in their fallen condition rather than take responsibility for their actions. Rather than mature into the things of God they want to be spoon fed and diaper attended for all of their choices.

They ask for others to extend them a measure of grace which will cover their nakedness, not knowing how Jesus already did this for them.[12] This calls into question whether what Jesus did was sufficient for them or not. By asking in this manner, over and over again, their actions demonstrate a hidden belief structure which hasn't received the fullness of the grace-gift presented to them in Jesus.

To further debilitate these people, there are those who succumb to the *"moral"* call of grace and extend these individuals the means to live in their mess without paying for the expense of inexperience, or

---

[12] For more on this, see my book *Grace for Shame – A Kingdom Solution for Reigning*

foolishness. While we are encouraged to come into the Kingdom as little children, we are not expected to live in that stunted form for very long. The following is an example of what I mean.

Jerry is a middle manager at a local distribution house. He has been a believer, attending his local church with his family for over thirty years. He recently was instrumental in getting Rainey a position in his department as his assistant. Rainey is a single mother who has been going to the same church as Jerry for the past three years. She was extremely grateful how Jerry helped her get this job since it brought an increase in pay which helped her make the ends meet for her and her son.

Recently, Jerry has been frustrated by the capabilities of Rainey to keep up with the pace of the work his department has been experiencing. While new duties haven't been assigned to her, the normal work demands of her position, which she quickly learned to accomplish, are now falling behind. At the end of day she is having to spend an extra hour after work just to get caught up. This is causing problems with her child care provider who expects Rainey to pick up her son at a certain time each day. But because she is late, an additional fee is being charged which is taking away funds for the other items they both need to make it through the week.

While these events have been transpiring, Rainey has become more agitated working with Jerry. Frequently she gets upset over the small details which he insists she must pay more attention to. It seems like everything is pressuring her to just quit. When Jerry asks her for a print out of the daily vouchers for the upcoming shift, she makes a mental note to get this to him. However, an hour later, when Jerry asks again in a more pressing manner, Rainey bursts out, *"Can you give me a little grace here?"*

Pressure always creates a burning desire for escape. Grace is not a relief valve to the pressure we experience. The result of grace will be a joyous exchange of honor which elevates.

Let's look at this example in practical terms. Because of their association at church, both Jerry and Rainey have certain social norms which they both operate from founded upon their shared belief. Jerry's assistance (favor) in getting Rainey hired in his department is a direct expression of their social norm to aid those less fortunate. Rainey's gratefulness to Jerry is her expression in the same social norm.

The business norms of Jerry's work require certain conditions to be met timely. There is built into these business norms performance requirements that define proficiency. While in the training period, Rainey advanced successfully towards these performance goals, she has only began recently to miss *"the mark"* of her profession. Failure to hit the mark creates pressure in Rainey to question her capabilities and whether she should continue working. Her outburst is an acknowledgment of her sin (missing the mark), and a plea to receive a benefit from their social norm in their business norm. Regrettably, what Rainey is crying out for is a crutch to enable her to rise to the occasion.

In the business norm, Rainey's plea is interpreted as, *"Back off, I'm drowning here with what I know. If you can do it better, then have it. Otherwise, remember how I performed in the past. You'll get what is coming when I'm able to give it."* (If you question this interpretation, recall the last time the phrase was used on you and how you interpreted it.)

Social and business norms are never the same. The flexibility found is social norms is often absent, on purpose, in business norms. Business norms expect, welcome, and are judged by profits. Social norms reject prophets (particularly in the church). How does this scenario look in the Kingdom if both people understand the operation of grace?

Jerry's frustration is a sign of how he has not found the grace-gift in Rainey working for the benefit of the department. This would mean speaking directly to her about what she feels is keeping the magnificence of the grace she holds from operating. Once determined, Jerry would draw upon the giftings within his department's *"grace-resources"* so the department could excel in its performance. This would enable Rainey to be a better contributor to accomplishing future goals.

While this example uses fictitious characters and scenarios, the principles behind it are very valid in a real-life application. The question is can you make the appropriate shift in how you view the operation of grace from a Kingdom mode?

Amazing Grace - the lie of an enemy

You and I have been lied to, duped, had the wool pulled over us, and any other form of manipulation which you can conjure up to explain the ruse of amazing grace. No I'm not talking about the grace which flows from the Kingdom of God, but the song, Amazing Grace. We have bought into a lie! Before you go and get your dander up let me explain.

THE HISTORY OF THE SONG.

The song Amazing Grace is probably one of the most world-wide recognizable songs. Its origination is from a poem which was written by John Newton for the Olney Hymns back in 1779. The story of John Newton is interesting in itself shown from this brief excerpt found on Wikipedia.

> Newton wrote the words from personal experience. He grew up without any particular religious conviction but his life's path was formed by a variety of twists and coincidences that were often put into motion by his recalcitrant insubordination. He was pressed into the Royal Navy and became a sailor, eventually participating in the slave trade. One night a terrible storm battered his vessel so severely that he became frightened enough to call out to God for mercy, a moment that marked the beginning of his spiritual conversion. His career in slave trading lasted a few years more until he quit going to sea altogether and began studying theology. [13]

The Olney Hymns were a collection of poems that Newton collaborated on with William Cowper as a means of presenting gospel material to the illiterate congregants of the community of Olney, England. It is believed this poem was an illustrative tool for a sermon which Newton delivered on January 1, 1773. It wasn't until later that the poem would be put to music. When this occurred, the song became almost the banner child for the 2nd Awakening in American.

THE LIE OF THE ENEMY

The popularity of such a song has caused over the centuries multitudes of peoples to commit their lives to Christ. Results like this are going to create a backlash from the powers of darkness in some form. So let's go see what a simple little change can make to wipe out all the work of the nature of grace. I've provided in the following chart the original poem as Newton wrote it and the lyrics which are sung across the globe today. Take a moment to read each so that you may see where the change has transpired.

Original Poem	Present Lyrics
Amazing grace! (how sweet the sound) That sav'd a wretch like me! I once was lost, but now am found, Was blind, but now I see.	Amazing Grace, how sweet the sound, That saved a wretch like me. I once was lost but now am found, Was blind, but now I see.
'Twas grace that taught my heart to fear, And grace my fears reliev'd; How precious did that grace appear The hour I first believ'd!	T'was Grace that taught my heart to fear. And Grace, my fears relieved. How precious did that Grace appear The hour I first believed.

---

[13] http://en.wikipedia.org/wiki/Amazing_Grace

Thro' many dangers, toils, and snares, I have already come; 'Tis grace hath brought me safe thus far, And grace will lead me home.	Through many dangers, toils and snares I have already come; 'Tis Grace that brought me safe thus far and Grace will lead me home.
The Lord has promis'd good to me, His word my hope secures; He will my shield and portion be As long as life endures.	The Lord has promised good to me. His word my hope secures. He will my shield and portion be, As long as life endures.
Yes, when this flesh and heart shall fail, And mortal life shall cease; I shall possess, within the veil, A life of joy and peace.	Yea, when this flesh and heart shall fail, And mortal life shall cease, I shall possess within the veil, A life of joy and peace.
The earth shall soon dissolve like snow, The sun forbear to shine; But God, who call'd me here below, Will be forever mine. *John Newton, Olney Hymns, 1779*	When we've been there ten thousand years Bright shining as the sun. We've no less days to sing God's praise Than when we've first begun.

The purposes of the enemy versus the nature of grace are diametrically opposed to one another. We are told that we are to be aware of the wiles of the enemy, meaning the subtle nature by which he works. Jesus has told us that the enemy is a liar and the father of all lies since the very beginning. This song is just one example of his works which we need to be aware of.

The ancient Greeks held the matter of grace very high and had three goddesses called the *Charites,* or *3 Graces,* which presided over the matters associated with grace. One of these areas the Greeks insisted grace encamped was in the song. They understood how music has the ability to instill honor through lyrics and/or melody. In such a manner, moments of conquest and valor could be passed on throughout the community for generations simply through a song. This passing of honor they understood to be one of the principles of grace.

Likewise, how many hymns have we sung about the greatness of God and the works He has accomplished through Jesus? This is a facet of grace we often have been ignorant of, or simply overlooked. Unfortunately, the enemy hasn't, nor would you expect him too, since his first job was the choir director in the realm of grace.

The Subtle Deception

By now you should have had opportunity to read both of these passages and see how the present day wording is pretty much unchanged - until you get to the last, or sixth stanza. This revision in the present song cannot be properly verified, and experts believe this stanza may not even have been part of the original song in the eighteenth century.

The first published rendition of this song's lyrics was found in Harriet Beecher Stowe's 1852 anti-slavery novel *Uncle Tom's Cabin* where Tom is said to sing this variation of the stanza as it was recalled from oral traditions passed down in African American communities. It came from a song called "Jerusalem. My Happy Home" found in a collection of verses originally published in 1790 in a book called *A Collection of Sacred Ballads.*

"Okay, what's the big deal? So they changed the lyrics. Who cares anyway?" is what I'm detecting now. Okay let's show you the big deal.

The sixth stanza starts: *"When we've been there ten thousand years..."* Where is there? Obviously, most respond, Heaven. Is that a true statement, will we be in Heaven for ten thousand years? If you have picked up anything about the grace of the Kingdom the answer should be obvious, but for those who are still uncommitted to this journey, let me instruct you in the ways of the kingdom.

> *That as sin hath reigned unto death, even so might grace reign through righteousness unto eternal life by Jesus Christ our Lord. (Romans 5:21)*

> *For the wages of sin is death; but the gift of God is eternal life through Jesus Christ our Lord. (Romans 6:23)*

I've already addressed this eternal life issue from the perspective of the Kingdom but it is still worth repeating. The verses above clearly state that eternal life is your grace reward. When does eternal life begin: at your death or at your belief in it? Obviously, this is a trick question. Eternal life is – it has no beginning or end. Yet it takes some people a while to grab a hold of the revelation that you are not going to die, you're not intended to die, you are eternal. Your eternal existence will be spent in one of two places – and this is where we deal with the issue of Heaven or hell. Have you read the back of the Bible? It truly has the answer on this matter.

> *And I saw a new heaven and a new earth: for the first heaven and the first earth were passed away; and there was no more sea. (2) And I John saw the holy city, new Jerusalem, coming down from God out of heaven, prepared as a bride adorned for her husband. **(3) And I heard a great voice out of heaven saying, Behold,***

the tabernacle of God is with men, and he will dwell with them, and they shall be his people, and God himself shall be with them, and be their God. (4) And God shall wipe away all tears from their eyes; and there shall be no more death, neither sorrow, nor crying, neither shall there be any more pain: for the former things are passed away. (5) And he that sat upon the throne said, Behold, I make all things new. And he said unto me, Write: for these words are true and faithful. (6) And he said unto me, It is done. I am Alpha and Omega, the beginning and the end. I will give unto him that is athirst of the fountain of the water of life freely. (7) He that overcometh shall inherit all things; and I will be his God, and he shall be my son. (8) But the fearful, and unbelieving, and the abominable, and murderers, and whoremongers, and sorcerers, and idolaters, and all liars, shall have their part in the lake which burneth with fire and brimstone: which is the second death. (Revelation 21:1-8)

Yes, this passage is in the Bible, go see for yourself. Man is not expected to live in Heaven but on Earth! God will come down to Earth and live among us. Heaven is the domain of angels while Earth is the domain of man. Therefore, the sixth stanza of the most popular song on the face of the Earth is a lie and you and I keep singing it. It is a lie, a lie, a bold faced lie! So are you ready for the rest of the story, the depth of a lie that just stinks of putrid filth?

THE ULTIMATE LIE

The sixth stanza shown to you is present day lyrics. Many of the older manuscripts which carry this stanza read as:

"When we've been here ten thousand years..."

Amazing isn't it? One little letter, which is shaped like a cross, changes the entire meaning of a song! Don't think for a moment that this subtle little ploy wasn't carefully crafted. Our enemy understands the power of song. He also knows the word of God and we saw him use it masterfully when he confronted Jesus. So why not take the one symbol which stripped him of his power and use it to take away the gift that God has given us?

Yes, the older versions of Amazing Grace had the biblical truth of man's plan to be eternal on Earth, at least 10,000 years! But one little lie, one little doubt, one little question of a truth sent swarms of believers into an early sleep. Look, Revelation 21:8 is fairly clear about who will be going into hell, and I am certainly not going to be known as an unbeliever simply because of a "t" in a word. I therefore, will do one of two things when Amazing Grace is played: I will sing the CORRECT RENDITION, or not sing at all.

What truly is amazing about grace is how you get this gift from God which gives you back the life you were intended to always possess, a life full of joy, a life which is abundant beyond your wildest imagination, and a life totally consumed with the presence of the Father. This is what grace provides. Do you believe it? The bigger question is: What will you do now since you know the rest of the story?

The Word of Grace

Are you a *"word"* person? Do you get all goose-pimply when going through the reference section of a book store? Is your favorite game 5+ letter Scrabble? Do you swoon at the thought of buying a new thesaurus? Do you have at least seven dictionaries bookmarked in your *"favorites"* folder on your computer or at least two word apps on your mobile phone? Let me take it to the next level: Do you own more than four Bibles? Do you find yourself highlighting passages out of the Strong's Concordance? Is your favorite biblical author W.E. Vines? If this describes you, then this section will be a treat to you. However, if you don't display any of these characteristics, fret not; you're still young, and *"He is faithful to complete that work which He started in you."*

WORDS OF TIME

One of the first items that I did on this subject of grace dealt with the *"time"* element of when grace began. We found from 2 Timothy 1:9 that grace actually comes from an eternal dimension and as such does not operate in the manner which time does.[14] Time as we recognize it today, and as it is defined in the New Testament, comes from the Greek Word *"chronos"* – it is the progressive passing of events in regulated intervals. We get the term *"chronological"* from this word. The sweeping of the second hand on your clock, the

---

[14] I covered this in the chapter entitled, Back in Time

flickering of LED diodes on your wristwatch, VCR and microwave, even the pages in your day-timer or the bank entries from your checking account are representative of this word.

Grace is not attached to this realm, it is eternal. This makes it an element of time known in the Greek as *"kairos"*, an intersection of the eternal realm into the *chronos*-based realm. But what example do you use to describe a *"kairos"* time event? They are varied, but for our purposes here, the most memorable one in each person's life is the day when we were born-again. At the moment you said yes to the Lordship of Jesus, *kairos* intersected *chronos* and you became a new creature who operates in both time zones. Cool, huh! Your word of agreement in a *chronos* environment opened the eternal realm and permitted the Father to reach into the earth and once again form a son and release the breath of His Spirit upon dust giving it the eternal life of the Kingdom of Heaven. Welcome to grace in *kairos*!

Why is it vital to understand this point? Remember the verse that Holy Spirit grabbed me with out of Ephesians which I mentioned in the opening chapter? Here is my amplified version again for you.

> *Let no rotten, time-based, foul or abusive words proceed out of your mouth but that which is intrinsically good and beneficial, suitable, as adorning a building with a new addition, properly designed with respect to the occupant's purpose and mission, in order that it may impart from the wealth of the abundance that you possess the joyously reciprocal gift of grace, thereby being and receiving encouragement to those that hear them. (Ephesians 4:29 amplified by mike)*

Look at the opening where it reads, *"Let no rotten, time-based..."* In the original it is the word *"corrupt"* which translated in the Greek means rotten. When something is described as rotten this means it is attached to *chronos*, or put another way, it has a date with death.

Rotten food is something which has passed its prime, it is decaying, and death is invading and consuming it. Its source of life has been severed and time has attached an appointment with corruption and death to it.

Here is another word which has a similar meaning. The word *"mortgage"* is a Spanish word that in its original meaning is defined as *"to the death."* How many of your words are mortgaged? Have you been trying to talk yourself out of situations which have been mortgaged by the very words you've spoken? These are not grace words. Any word which is tied to time is mortgaged and you don't own it − it owns you and is extracting the life that is backing it as payment. Words filled with grace are timeless. They have contained within them the ability to give life and give it in abundance. How do I know this? From these two verses.

In the beginning was the Word, and the Word was with
God, and the Word was God. (John 1:1)

The thief cometh not, but for to steal, and to kill, and to
destroy: I am come that they might have life, and that
they might have it more abundantly. (John 10:10)

LET'S TALK ABOUT THE WORD

The book of Proverbs tells us life and death are in the power of the tongue. Notice that it doesn't say one or the other but rather both. The book of James tells us that we are the ones who control our tongue and if we don't, our tongue will control us like a bit in a horse's mouth. So we need to come to a proper Kingdom understanding of our words and the power they contain when we release them. In order for this to occur, yes, we need to go back to the beginning. Oh! Wait a minute; we were just there in John 1

"In the beginning was the Word. . ." couple this with 2 Timothy 1:9 and we know any word which was in the beginning was operating out of grace according to the purpose of the Father. So the question that begs to be asked is: What was the first recorded eternal word spoken in grace? Do you know? Let's go find out.

> *In the beginning God created the heaven and the earth. (2) And the earth was without form, and void; and darkness was upon the face of the deep. And the Spirit of God moved upon the face of the waters. (3) And God said, Let there be light: and there was light. (Genesis 1:1-3)*

(I admit that I have been leading you around in this for a while.) *"Let. . ."* is the first recorded word by God and isn't it amazing how it is also the first word in this passage from Ephesians 4:29 we're addressing here. Wouldn't this mean there is something significant about this word? (If you don't think so, play along just to entertain me.) This word has greatness backing it and we never even realized it. Sure it might have triple word value in a game of Scrabble but I'm talking bigger meaning here. Let (there it is again!) me take you to an explanation of this word's meaning which I found:

> *"Let may imply a positive giving of permission but more often implies failure to prevent either through inadvertence and negligence or through lack of power or authority." Webster's Seventh Collegiate Dictionary*

In the use of this word we see that permission is given to carry out an order, yet this order is conducted on the basis of a purposeful act of power and authority. The word has within it the nature to release any manner of restraint and give full, unhindered opportunity to carry out its assignment based on the authority behind its use. So whenever God said, *"Let..."* He was releasing an authoritative word which would go unhindered and uninterrupted to accomplish its determined assignment. This is what it means when God says in Isaiah 55 that His word will not come back to Him void, it will accomplish that which it was sent to do. This is the inherent nature of a grace-filled word – it cannot come back void. *"But how is that possible?"* is what I'm hearing.

Look at Genesis 1:2 again. Notice how the Earth was without form and void. The void was already present. Anything coming from a dimension which contains abundance is going to displace the emptiness in this void. It can't be stopped. If the element which enters the void is full of life, it will, by its very nature, abound in the characteristics of life and produce after itself overwhelming the void until all which remains is abundant life. We know from basic science that life does not progressively grow one upon another (i.e. 1+1+1+1+1) but grows exponentially (i.e. 1+1+2+4+8). You've got to understand how the **only** thing which stood out in this void was the potential of a word to go to work since nothing else would.

Whenever I read this passage I envision the Trinity tossing a football around creation. Holy Spirit is hovering around preparing to run a route which is commenced at the Father's word, *"Let. . ."* Whatever follows this word is the passing of the football (Jesus, the Word) to Holy Spirit who will catch the word (Jesus) and see that the score is made. The beauty of this is how there are no defenders trying to block Holy Spirit from receiving the football (Jesus). The result is ALWAYS a score. Do you now understand the power of a grace-filled word?

We not only need to recognize and understand the power of *"Let..."* but we need to live it as well. Why would I say this? Go to Genesis 1:26.

And God said, Let us make man in our image, after our likeness: and let them have dominion over the fish of the sea, and over the fowl of the air, and over the cattle, and over all the earth, and over every creeping thing that creepeth upon the earth. (Genesis 1:26)

Our very creation and purpose was established by the word *"Let."* Do not pull that, *"This only applies to the creation of Adam,"* excuse on me! It says in Ephesians we were in Him before the foundation of the world, and it also says that God speaks those things that be not as though they were, and He knows the end from the beginning. So the very release of the word *"Let. . ."* in this verse set you and I into motion towards God's purpose. As a matter of truth, every one of us were a word in God's mouth waiting for *"Let. . ."* to set us on an unhindered and uninterrupted journey towards the plan and purpose of God.

"But my life has been everything but unhindered and uninterrupted," is the moaning I'm hearing now. Stop for a moment. I'm serious, stop! Notice the last three words which you read. What were they?

1) I'm serious, stop!

2) that you read

3) What were they?

4) You've lost me!

I pray that you didn't answer this matter with number 4! The point of this small exercise is two-fold: 1.) Sometimes you need to stop and look to see the forest through the trees, metaphorically speaking; 2.) In each occurrence there is an underlying order or pattern for the words. Is it possible that you're life is not in alignment with the sentence which God spoke about you. Put another way, maybe you're not with the right set of words, or maybe the words you're associated with haven't matured yet.

Consider this: Children when they are very young don't speak like adults. Their language skills display the exploratory nature of their world – basically they clunk around with language like they clunk around the yard. As they experience more things their language develops to describe those occurrences better and more accurately. Example: How often have you asked a five-year old what they did for the day and were then confronted with a detailed, moment by moment explanation of their experiences of the day, whereas when you ask the same question to a 15-year old, their response is, *"Nothing?"*

ASSOCIATING WITH...LIFE!

In our example verse from Ephesians 4:29, we have a directive issued in *"Let..."* which is associated with life by the word *"no."* "No," we have all recognized from a very early age is negative. So anything which follows it is negative. But remember in your math class when your teacher would ask you the most ridiculous question in the world, *"What is the result when two negatives are put together?"* Two negatives! Who ever heard of such a thing? This is such a thing! No Corrupt. Two negatives. So the answer to the question your teacher asked is...Yes, a positive! The mathematical answer is, ***"No Corrupt = Life!"*** *"But I thought we were talking about words not math!"*

Good point. Words have the ability to have their meaning changed by associating with a prefix or suffix. How can this change a living word? *"Living"* can be cut short by an *"ed"* and become *"lived"* or lose its nature by *"less"* and be *"lifeless."* The birth of a word can be terminated before its delivery and be *"still born."* Some words (people) feel limited. Their meaning can be changed instantly when they team up with a *"un"* and become *"unlimited."* Just look at the directive of *"Let..."* which is *"unhindered"* and *"uninterrupted."* If you're feeling either hindered or interrupted then you need to find a *"un"* to move you back into your purpose. This is a very delicate situation though because a word which is *"known"* who teams up with a *"un"* suddenly becomes *"unknown."* So you have to ask yourself, *"Self. What prefix or suffix has attached a negative to my word?"*

So let (there it is again!) me bring this portion to a close. We have discovered,

- A grace-filled word expressed into a void will overwhelm the void with abundant life.

- A grace-filled word is a word that isn't attached to the *chronos* time of this world but to the *kairos* time of the eternal realm from which it comes.

- *"Let..."* causes an event to occur which operates unhindered and uninterrupted with power and authority that stands behind the directive.

- One negative word can be changed by attaching it to another negative word creating a positive change.

- The word of grace has the nature to release all manner of restraint to carry out its assignment based on the authority behind its intended purpose.

- All of us were a grace-word on the lips of God and we were released into His plan and purpose when He declared, *"Let..."*

So I'll ask the question asked me from a great man of God, Dr. Fizer: Are you living the *"Let"* yet?

WORDS OF GRACE PART II

All words – written, as well as spoken - have causative effect. They create. They take on, or become life. The form of this life is determined by the order or pattern of the words and the thought they are trying to convey. More words do not clarify – they abound around the nature of the life given in the original words.

WORDS AS BUILDING BLOCKS

> Let no corrupt speech proceed out of your mouth, but such
> as is good for edifying as the need may be, that it may
> give grace to them that hear. (Ephesians 4:29)

In this passage the word "speech" is the Greek term *logos*. Strong Concordance defines this word as:

Something said (including the thought); by implication a topic (subject of discourse), also reasoning (the mental faculty) or motive; by extension a computation; specifically (with the article in John) the Divine Expression (that is, Christ)

Thayer's Dictionary has a much more comprehensive definition for *logos* but as I've already stated, more words do not clarify. So *logos* is a word, or words, which convey an intended, orderly thought in the course of speaking. In the book of John we also discover that Jesus is described as the Word or *logos*.

> In the beginning was the Word, and the Word was with
> God, and the Word was God. (John 1:1)

> In the beginning God created the heaven and the earth.
> (2) And the earth was without form, and void; and
> darkness was upon the face of the deep. And the Spirit
> of God moved upon the face of the waters. (3) And God

said, Let there be light: and there was light. (Genesis 1:1-3)

So in these two passages we see that *logos* created all things. God ruling and reigning from the eternal realm of grace issues a decree, speaks a word, utters a sound, whatever figure of speech you wish to employ, and things begin to come into order and alignment over the chaos which was upon the deep. We are told in scripture that God cannot lie. The reason is simple according to John 1:1 – God and His word are one, they are integrated. Look at God and you see His Word; look at His word and you see God. There is no space for anything else. If God said that you will have a three-headed, blue Doberman dog outside your door in the morning, you can be certain it will happen. Why? Because His word creates all it says it will create.

There is an important caveat to this explanation which must be understood: This dog will only show up if it is in the plan and purpose which God has intended for your life. God only issues a word which has been carefully created to follow a predetermined purpose, a purpose which always reflects the nature of His kingdom, and conversely, His nature also. His inability to lie is only because if He did, He being associated with a lie, would make Himself to be a lie too. Therein lies the strength of the word of God – it lives just as He lives. This is why He declares in the book of Isaiah 55 that His word shall not come back to Him void, or useless. Coming from a realm of grace, which is full of abundant life, every single word produces. So let's look at my amplified version to our main passage from Ephesians 4:29 again.

Let no rotten, time-based, foul or abusive words proceed out of your mouth but that which is intrinsically good and beneficial, suitable, as adorning a building with a new addition, properly designed with respect to the occupant's purpose and mission, in order that it may impart from the wealth of the abundance that you possess the joyously reciprocal gift of grace, thereby being and receiving encouragement to those that hear them. (Ephesians 4:29 amplified by mike)

I want to take a moment here to explain the word in the original which is *"edify"* and compare it with my version. The Greek word we see as *"edify"* is *"oikodomē"* and it is a compound word which has the meaning of a dwelling with a roof. Obviously, we don't go around extolling the virtues of someone's house and its roof, right? The point Paul is trying to make here is how the thought and intention of words act the same way that walls and roofs do – they have to work together towards a purpose.

This is what Paul is trying to convey: The order of purpose comes to the believer from the inside by the work of Holy Spirit. The design of the structure is intended to span across multiple conditions and be solidly anchored at critical points where the daily stress has been properly founded on the secure nature of stone pediments.

This is an example of what a word of grace does. It builds from the inside out. It is orderly yet life fulfilling. A grace word will strip away a false facade but replace it with a portico, or covered entrance, which welcomes others into the splendor of the kingdom while protecting them from the elements.

"That sounds eloquent, Mike, but I can't see myself doing this." Well here is your choice then.

The thief cometh not, but for to steal, and to kill, and to destroy: I am come that they might have life, and that they might have it more abundantly. (John 10:10)

Which do you chose? Yes, you do have a choice – words of life or words of death. We need to understand that there is the same power in every word we speak as in the very words which God spoke. If you don't believe this, then look at this very familiar passage.

> *And God said, Let us make man in our image, after our likeness: and let them have dominion... (Genesis 1:26)*

Our creation, as I wrote, came with the word *"Let. . ."* Our form and nature is based on the pattern of the God-head itself. Our purpose is defined again with *"Let..."* which clearly determines the strength of our words. Dominion required the ability to rule with words which can be followed. All of our words carry the same power which God's words possess since we are made in His image and likeness. *"Are you saying that we're God?!!!"* That subject is such a powder keg which requires skillful handling, so going fully into it requires a whole separate book. For now, if you are made in His image and likeness, if your purpose is to have dominion on the Earth, if His Spirit lives inside of you evidenced with the speaking of a heavenly language, if you are seated in heavenly places while being the temple of God on Earth, THEN there is a power to your words which grace has influenced.

WORDS OF GRACE PART III

In the first part of this chapter we looked at what it means to let no corrupt speech out of your mouth. The second part dealt with the concept of words which are building blocks. In both of these parts the life giving nature of grace is the basis of their purpose. In this final part we look at the giving aspect.

A GIFT OF GRACE FROM...

I am often asked how someone gives grace to another. This is a tricky subject to address simply because it requires a person understanding how there are two levels of grace in operation at all times: The grace of this world and the grace of the Kingdom of God. To ask how you give grace to someone requires you to know what the differences are between the two and then determine which you wish to deposit into someone.

Understand when man fell in the garden, he fell from the eternal Kingdom of grace into a worldly, time-based grace which he would control. The grace of this world operates in the fashion of, *"I'll give to you as long as it suits my needs and satisfaction,"* or *"I'll be joyful as long as you don't do something that offends me."* Jesus came to give us the Kingdom back and the grace which operates from it. Hence, grace of this world for the true grace of the Kingdom. John even indicates the difference in John 1:16 at the beginning of the verse with, *". . . his fullness have all we received..."* speaking of the abundance which is produced from the Kingdom operating from grace which is lacking in a worldly, time-based system.

I recognize most people asking how to give grace don't think they are going to be giving grace associated with the world system, yet when I explain the differences to them, they suddenly become aware how the grace they have grown up around has been conditional – a fact which violates the grace of the Kingdom of God. I know this from this passage out of Luke.

> *"But I say to you who hear: Love your enemies, do good to those who hate you, (28) bless those who curse you, and pray for those who spitefully use you. (29) To him who strikes you on the one cheek, offer the other also. And from him who takes away your cloak, do not withhold your tunic either. (30) Give to everyone who asks of you. And from him who takes away your goods do not ask them back. (31) And just as you want men to do to you, you also do to them likewise. (32) "But if you love those who love you, what credit is that to you? For even sinners love those who love them. (33) And if you*

do good to those who do good to you, what credit is that to you? For even sinners do the same. (34) And if you lend to those from whom you hope to receive back, what credit is that to you? For even sinners lend to sinners to receive as much back. (35) But love your enemies, do good, and lend, hoping for nothing in return; and your reward will be great, and you will be sons of the Most High. For He is kind to the unthankful and evil. (36) Therefore be merciful, just as your Father also is merciful. (Luke 6:27-36)

When I spoke to you about the reciprocal nature of grace, I brought verse 31 to you as an example of this nature, knowing that I had pulled it out of the entire context of its passage. My point was to demonstrate what the Greeks understood about *charis*, or grace. This entire passage from Luke demonstrates the giving nature of grace from the Kingdom perspective. From the perspective of the Kingdom of God, grace when given in the world system is characterized in verse 36 as being merciful.

I stated previously how mercy is the action from the Kingdom which moves you back into the environment of grace.[15] Most people don't operate from a position of Kingdom grace, so when you're trying to impart this manner of grace to them, it just *"flies over their head."* In this passage from Luke, Jesus is telling us not everyone is going to appreciate your *"grace"* effort. He wants you to respond to these people just as your Father would, operating from *chesed*, but displaying mercy – expecting nothing in return – so they may be able to move eventually into the realm of Kingdom grace. When you expect nothing in return, you have just removed the conditional nature of the world's grace out from underneath them. This move makes an impact in their life – guaranteed. The reciprocal nature of

---

[15] Found in the chapter, "Hebrew to Greek and Back Again"

grace also insures that you experience a similar impact, but on a different level. If you doubt me on this matter, do the following: The next time you go to purchase a coffee or hamburger, lay down an additional $10.00 and tell the clerk that it is to pay for whoever is behind you for whatever they order until it runs out. Then leave without saying anything to the person(s) behind you. I assure you what you'll experience at that moment will be beyond anything this world has given you.

The Sons of Grace

We are in tumultuous times. Wars and rumors of war splash across the screens of our smart phones, tablets, computers and TV's. We have witnessed devastation on a scale which boggles the mind. Local economies splinter into smaller units only to be eaten up by larger multi-national organizations. There is unrest in nations who have never worried about it in the past. People are concerned about their food, their health, and their very way of life. The entire planet is straining for one thing: The manifestation of the Sons of God.

Sure I could quote a very familiar passage out of Romans 8 which speaks to the sons of God, but I want to go to a verse spoken by Jesus himself that addresses the matter I feel better than from Paul.

> *Be perfect, therefore, as your heavenly Father is perfect.*
> *(Matthew 5:48)*

This statement comes from a portion of the beatitudes where Jesus has just described the nature of grace as the Kingdom of God sees it. The point I want to make here is how Jesus clearly states we have the ability to be perfect in the same manner our Father in Heaven is perfect. But what does it mean to be perfect? The Greek word is *teleios* and it means to be of full age, mature. The contrast to this term would be a *"babe"* in Christ. It implies a goal or destination - it is not a pass into Heaven. Not for one moment do I want you to think Jesus is saying you only become this when you get to Heaven. His statement ends a very long passage about acts which are carried out here on Earth, not in Heaven. So clearly, according to Jesus, on Earth, we can be perfect as our Father is.

SON OR HEIR

I want to explore deeper the two Greek words for son and what their difference is according to how the Apostles John and Paul use them.[16] The first is the word *teknon* and this word describes the son who is birthed. It can denote what disciples are called by their teacher. This is the term Mary used to describe her son, Jesus. The second Greek word is *huios* and its difference in meaning is how it is based upon a matter of relationship with the parent. This is the term Jesus used exclusively to describe His relationship with the Father and it is this type of son which Jesus is calling us to enter into from out of Matthew 5:48.

> *He came unto his own, and his own received him not. (12) But as many as received him, to them gave he power to become the sons of God, even to them that believe on his name: (13) Which were born, not of blood, nor of the will of the flesh, nor of the will of man, but of God. (John 1:11-13)*

> *Behold, what manner of love the Father hath bestowed upon us, that we should be called the sons of God: therefore the world knoweth us not, because it knew him not. (2) Beloved, now are we the sons of God, and it doth not yet appear what we shall be: but we know that, when he shall appear, we shall be like him; for we shall see him as he is. (1 John 3:1-2)*

---

[16] I mentioned this back in the chapter, "Grace is Not..."

In these two passages John is describing our birth as *teknon* of God. He sees us as small children born from the Father. If you are born again, you are describing yourself as *teknon*. Paul even employs this term in Romans 8 as he describes our birth in the Spirit.

> *The Spirit itself beareth witness with our spirit, that we are the **children** of God: (17) And if **children**, then heirs; heirs of God, and joint-heirs with Christ; if so be that we suffer with him, that we may be also glorified together. (Romans 8:16-17)*

Being a *teknon* is our heritage in Christ through the work of rebirth in the Spirit. Many believers unfortunately stay here, hanging out in their diapers crying out for God to put their binkie back in their mouth so they'll feel safe again. *"God help me with..."* and, *"God, why am I..."* and, *"God, you need to..."* are the common cries of a *teknon* trying to fit into the world around them. The dilemma is that a *teknon* hasn't reached *teleios* (maturity) to understand you don't fit into this world – you take authority over it. As Paul said,

> *For as many as are led by the Spirit of God, they are the **sons** of God. (Romans 8:14)*

> *For the earnest expectation of the creature waiteth for the manifestation of the **sons** of God. (Romans 8:19)*

Each occurrence here in these passages is *huios*, a son who has a relationship with Holy Spirit and the Father. This relationship provides to you all the benefits Jesus declared when He stated that He only did what He saw the Father do or say what He heard the Father say. It is out of this relationship, a relationship which is defined by Paul as *"being in Christ"* that you are to manifest yourself for all of creation. A *huios* is someone who is *teleios* (mature) in the things of the Spirit, someone who knows the Father's heart and operates in His ways. When those people begin to appear on the Earth, things will start to happen which most people will call miraculous, but it really will be just the nature of the Kingdom of grace being displayed on Earth, as it is in Heaven.

> *Therefore be imitators of God, as beloved children, (Ephesians 5:1)*

> *Be ye therefore merciful, as your Father also is merciful. (Luke 6:36)*

In these passages Paul starts off telling us to imitate God as a *teknon*. This is the manner in which all children do the things they see their parents do. Nothing is more adorable than watching your child put on your shoes or hat and pretend they are you. We all love it and there are a multitude of photo albums which have been produced to hold the records of such events. Heaven has the same type of photo book which displays all the times you acted like the Father.

Remember, when you read Luke 6:36, if there is any mention of mercy, grace is standing right next to it. The Father and all of creation are waiting for mature sons to manifest on Earth and begin demonstrating "on Earth as it is in Heaven." There will be no more need for the Earth to groan for deliverance because the *huios* will be present with liberty. So what are you waiting for? *Teleios*.

FULL OF GRACE AND TRUTH

In this study of grace I've tried to show the facets we have missed in our religious upbringing in order to prepare us to be able to rule and reign with Christ when the time comes. This is after all what the Father is looking towards and His plan hasn't changed since He enacted it before the foundations of the world. Most people get all excited about the thought of ruling with Christ, but when the rubber meets the road, they don't have a clue on how this will be done. And if you don't know how it will be done, how would you even know what the environment would look like to do it in? This is part of the reason for this book – to describe the environment so you'll know how to operate when the time comes. It's not good enough knowing about grace but how to function in grace.

When you understand it is the intention of the Father to see you rule with Jesus, you're going to have to recognize what it means to be "in Christ." Yes, this is an identification issue which every believer must secure for themselves, but it is also the manner by which all of your actions will be acknowledged both for, and from, the Kingdom. Since Jesus is our pattern, we need to look to Him and see what the Father sees in Him which He also sees in us.

> *And the Word was made flesh, and dwelt among us, (and we beheld his glory, the glory as of the only begotten of the Father,) full of grace and truth. (15) John bare witness of him, and cried, saying, This was he of whom I spake, He that cometh after me is preferred before me: for he was before me. (16) And of his fulness have all we received, and grace for grace. (17) For the law was given by Moses, but grace and truth came by Jesus Christ. (John 1:14-17)*

Previously, I spoke about the Word, or *logos* in the Greek. This passage is the identification of the manifestation of God's spoken word in the bodily form we recognize as Jesus. What is unique about this identity is the connection of *"full of grace and truth."* Nowhere in the Bible do we have a description of what Jesus looks like but only the characteristics which He displayed. I think we need to look at the connection of *"full of grace and truth"* and how these influenced His actions both with people and the Father.

Notice in verse 14 we have what is called a parenthetical statement: A remark which is contained within parenthesis that can be viewed as independent of the main content or, for clarification purposes, added as a descriptor. For the moment I want to remove it from the context of this matter and in doing so the verse would subsequently read, *"And the Word was made flesh, and dwelt among us, full of grace and truth."*

While I'm in a grammatical mode, let me briefly review the meaning of the word *"and."* This word is known as a conjunction with the purpose of joining two or more simple sentences together in order to make them flow better for the reader. It also performs the function of joining elements together to provide a fuller description of the whole. I mention this since I know someone is going to take issue with my removing the parenthetical statement in order to advance the next element.

"...full of grace and truth..." is a conjunctive description of grace, meaning that *"...full of grace..."* indicates quantity while *"...and truth..."* indicates the quality of the grace. This means the grace which Jesus demonstrated in his life was always full and of the purest form. The notion of a grace which isn't pure may seem odd but this is what verse 16 is indicating. The phrase *"grace for grace"* indicates there was a form of grace present which was replaced by the grace that Jesus possessed.

THE PICTURE OF GRACE

In the entire gospel of John, these opening verses are the only places where the word *"grace"*, or *charis* in the Greek, is used. This overall depiction of Jesus is what John will, through the remaining chapters, unfold bit by bit, until we reach the end where John admits he only wrote those things which would lead you to believe Jesus is the Son of God, and have life in His name.

What is interesting in these verses we have been examining is the picture they create when brought all together. In verse 14 the word *"dwelt"* represents a tent, or in Hebrew it would be called a *"tabernacle."* So when you look at the entire sentence, including the parenthetical statement, there is an amazing picture Holy Spirit is creating through John's words. It harkens back to a time when Israel wandered in the wilderness; God daily communed with them from His tabernacle which dwelt in their midst. Everyone in the camp knew when God was in His tabernacle by the glory cloud which hovered over the tent of meeting. In this tent, Moses would speak to God, come back to the children of Israel and repeat what God had told him - conversations which would become known as the Law.

John tells us in these few opening verses that as great as it was for the children of Israel in the wilderness with God, Jesus provided something far greater – a tangible presence available to all, and with that presence, access to the Kingdom of God which the children of Israel never knew. Yes, the Law was important. It established the protocol of how to enter into the presence of God, but it lacked the ability to instill the life essence which abounds in a Kingdom established around grace. All of the rituals and sacrifices point to the one who would give life rather than take it and this is the truth God wanted all men to know.

This is the pattern we seek to represent to the world: the fullness of grace and truth in our daily activities. It is not a grace many have deemed unmerited favor, but a grace which is joyous and giving in all aspects of life. It is abundant in its very nature, overwhelming the need and lack which parade around it. This is our heritage. This is where we reign from, "...in Christ." Are you up to the challenge?

Living in Grace

Is it possible to live in grace like that environment which exists in Heaven? Yes. Yet many think it can't happen until they arrive in Heaven. The question to ask about such a mind-set is why would Jesus direct the disciples to pray, *". . .your kingdom come, your will be done, **on earth as it is in heaven**,"* or *". . . seek first the kingdom of God and His righteousness..."* if it wasn't possible?

The Kingdom of Grace is expected to return back to Earth – even the creation knows that it's coming, which is why it is groaning for the manifestation of the sons of God. To be given the title of a *"Son of God"* means you have lived in the environment which surrounds God: breathed in its richness; seen its vastness; and experienced its overwhelming peace and joy. As a Son you are able to bring this environment into every area of your life simply because you live there. It is a vital part of your DNA.

In this chapter I'm going to unveil a greater picture of the Kingdom of Grace and bring it into our daily lives. The Genesis account of creation and the events leading up to the fall of man are familiar to most. Too often we view these first couple of chapters through a lens filtered by the effects of the sin man committed. When we do this we miss out on the expressions and even the very environment which flows from grace.

The 5 Grace Keys

As I begin this, let me bring previous lessons together and present the following keys of grace. From these I trust you'll be able to recognize the prevalence of grace around us.

1) Grace is eternal.

2) Grace is reciprocal giving.

3) Grace produces pleasure.

4) Grace abounds.

5) Grace leaves thanksgiving in its wake.

In the Beginning

Every event starts with something. What did creation start with? If you jump in here and say God spoke, then I must unfortunately tell you that you are wrong. Yes, the opening passage says God spoke, but this is only a record of what transpired at the start of creation – it is not the beginning. Scriptures tells us God knows the end from the beginning so this means in order for God to start creation, He had to see what the end looked like. All of creation is subsequently manufactured to the specification of the part it will contribute to the final, completed picture.

We do not know the duration of *"time"* it took God to design this project of creation, but before the foundations were laid, the planning of all we experience was being considered in the realm of grace. Every thought, every intersection of eternity with time, every effect from the choices of freewill was carefully taken into account with the environment of grace influencing it.

Long before a single word was spoken to start creation, grace was pulsating with life-giving potential. This is the true meaning of Divine

Grace, not the theological definition of unmerited favor we have been indoctrinated in. We were in God's thoughts long before sin entered this world. His intention to have a family stands as the pinnacle within the realm of grace and is the operator behind all of creation.

We discover in Proverbs 8, John 1, and Colossians 2 the role Jesus played in the designing and construction process of creation. He too, operating from the realm of grace, prepared a place for us which would serve towards the final, complete picture. His declaration to the disciples that Holy Spirit would come upon them was not a *"stop-gap"* measure to a failed fulfillment of destiny, but a calculated act from the Kingdom of grace made in eternity past. Every salvation has been carefully and skillfully considered in a realm where the nature of living in abundance forever is *"natural"* not super-natural.

In this eternal realm of grace, miracles never happen – wholeness is natural. Have you ever considered that God has never experienced a miracle? Miracles point to God and He doesn't need to experience a miracle to confirm to Him that He is. When you live in the realm of grace you don't experience miracles – you experience the *"normal"* life of the realm. Those who aren't from this realm will see miracles occur in their lives as you intersect with them. If you're longing to experience a miracle this tells me that you don't desire to live from the realm of grace but out of mercy. The purpose of mercy is to point you to grace, where you are to live continually, rather than until you need your next *"fix"* of mercy.

Just as there are no miracles in the realm of grace, we must also come to the understanding how needs and wants do not exist in this environment too. A need and want represents a lack which is contradictory in a realm teaming with abundance. This property of grace is continually supplied to us in Christ, even unto the end of the age, and was figured into the plan of creation.

Consider that when you live from the realm of grace, blind eyes open, food is multiplied, limbs grow back, fish become a purse with gold coins for you, you ruin every funeral you attend, and so much more. This is the pre-planned life which is backed from a realm which gets tremendous joy out of you being a part of it. Those around you will think that because these things happen around you, that you have the characteristic known as *"favor."* Favor denotes special consideration beyond *"normal"* conditions, but what they don't know is that this **IS** normal for you. Favor is your way of recognizing grace is operating in your life.

When you read *"In the beginning. . ."* from this point on realize everything which I've just touched upon is contained in those words, plus a whole lot more which is still being unfolded to us. You and I were in the *"In"* where grace reigns. To us, as heirs, abounds all which this realm contains and manifests, not in a time to come, but now, this very moment and every moment which follows. This is what it means to live in the beginning, before the foundations of time, where grace under-girds the purpose you live. This is His gift to you.

THE GOODNESS OF GRACE

So let's go back to the beginning again to look at the description of the nature to grace as it has been recorded in the Hebrew text. *Charis* is the Greek term which in the New Testament is interpreted as *"grace,"* and yet its definition is different from the Hebrew word of *"chên"* which is often listed as *"grace"* in the Old Testament. Some scholarly types would say if there is going to be any teaching on grace, you should start with the definition from the Hebrew since it was first given to them through the Law of Moses.

I respect this position, and yet, it is the Greek writings, in the New Testament, which clearly states grace existed before the foundations of the world (2 Tim. 1:9; Eph. 1:4-6). Furthermore, the Apostle John clearly states in the first chapter of his gospel how the Law came by Moses but that grace came by Jesus. I agree that both need to be addressed, if not for their differences alone, at least for their similarities. This, regrettably to you purveyors of the Word, isn't where I am being directed in this study presently.

What I believe is important is to be able to take what we have learned from the Greek text and see if we can identify similar signposts as they appear in another language. If I was to ask you to describe the concept of light, an important factor throughout the entire Bible, you would have to make mention of not only its property of brilliance and radiance it possesses but you would also have to contrast this property against darkness and shadows. The same topic would still not be complete if you neglected to mention the nature of color and how it is produced by the interplay of light and the cellular structure of an object.

The manifold nature of grace requires similar treatment when you begin looking at it from the perspective of the Kingdom of God. I'm going to focus more on the patterns found in the Hebrew text using the filters we established from the Greek interpretations of *charis*. However, to establish a pattern, we need to know what we're looking for.

> But rather seek ye the kingdom of God; and all these things shall be added unto you. (32) Fear not, little flock; for it is your Father's good pleasure to give you the kingdom. (Luke 12:31-32)

> Having made known unto us the mystery of his will, according to his good pleasure which he hath purposed in himself: (Ephesians 1:9)

Our pattern is the Father's good pleasure and how it is displayed in the creation events. Recall that *charis* has a root meaning which encompasses all the facets of joy. I don't ever recall a time in my life when joy was not pleasurable, do you? I also don't recall when something which I felt pleasure with wasn't good, do you? So if we can find *"pleasure,"* we'll probably find *"good,"* and conversely if we find *"good,"* we'll find *"pleasure."*

I recognize this concept is simple to articulate – most of the Kingdom is this way – but you'd be amazed at how many people have never thought this through for themselves, and unfortunately missed so much of what the narrative is speaking to us about. I think the enemy has kept us so bound up in our *"past sin nature"* that we're fearful of what God really has prepared for us. We're afraid God is going to smack us with a heavenly baseball bat any time we do anything which might be the least bit *"unholy"* (a definition which runs the gambit from drinking to wearing makeup). This keeps us in "check" with the enemy, but out of the vast wealth the Father has laid up for us to inherit. So my intention is to set you free from the restrictions which you've allowed the enemy, or past teachings, to place upon you.

YOUR FATHER'S GOOD PLEASURE

The first two chapters of the Genesis account of creation is, along with the last chapter of Revelation, the best parts of the Bible, since only these chapters declare the intent of the Father for all of us. Everything in between is how mankind messed it up and God fixed it. So if you truly understand just these three chapters of the Bible, you know the intent of God for your life. (I'm going to catch a lot of flak from certain people for this statement, so please don't write me about it since I told you so.)

In the first chapter of Genesis we find the creative work of God being expressed through His words and how they fashioned the universe and all of its contents. It is here that we're going to find if our *"pleasure pattern"* exists as I've established it. Here are the opening verses from Genesis which most of us are familiar with.

> *In the beginning God created the heaven and the earth. (2) And the earth was without form, and void; and darkness was upon the face of the deep. And the Spirit of God moved upon the face of the waters. (3) And God said, Let there be light: and there was light. (4) And God saw the light, that it was good: and God divided the light from the darkness. (5) And God called the light Day, and the darkness he called Night. And the evening and the morning were the first day. (Genesis 1:1-5)*

In these verses we find a number of things, but I'm focusing on the creation of light on the first day. Even though this is an interpretation from the original Hebrew text we're peering into, you still can see that it has many of the same characteristics every language has in trying to convey a message. The signpost which we're looking for in this text has to do with pleasure, so the question is do you see where this may be located? If you do, how did you locate this pleasure of the Father?

For those who still are having some difficulty, allow me to open your eyes for understanding here. The pleasure the Father is having is located in verse four, *"God saw the light, that it was good: and God divided the light from the darkness."* The word that signifies He is having pleasure is the word *"good."* (I said this was simple!)

In English terms the word *"good"* is an adjective when associated with the word *"pleasure"* as shown in our passages out of Luke 12:37 and Ephesians 1:9. This means that *"good"* modifies, or intensifies, the nature of *"pleasure"*. However, here in the Hebrew text, it is an adverb, modifying the nature of an action. I make mention of this for one simple reason: The Hebrew language is very active in its construction. Greek, and subsequently English, follows the pattern of noun/verb while the Hebrew text often follows the pattern of verb/noun. So just what does this word "good" mean in the Hebrew? *Tobe* is the Hebrew word and its adjective definition in the Strong's Concordance says,

> *beautiful, best, better, bountiful, cheerful, at ease, fair, favour, fine, glad, good (deed, -lier, liest, -ly, -ness, -s), graciously, joyful, kindly, kindness, like (best), loving, merry, most, pleasant, pleaseth, pleasure, precious, prosperity, ready, sweet, wealth, welfare, well favoured.*

So in this definition we begin to see the nature of grace with the words of pleasure, good, joyful, favour and of course, graciously, plus a whole wealth of other terms which we haven't even begun to delve into. Every occurrence of the word *"good"* in the Old Testament contains within it these terms, all of which define the word, and conversely, any one of these terms used in the text would also represent the nature of *"good."*

THE CORNERSTONE OF GRACE

While I'm highlighting these first few verses, I want to draw your attention to a very important aspect of the nature of grace. Something which I can say is the cornerstone to how it operates. Notice verse 5 [17] which called the light day and the darkness night. Pretty standard stuff, right? But notice the way God orders the day in the remaining part of the verse: The evening and the morning were the first day. In our Western culture our days begin at the crack of dawn where we hustle off to do our business and end at sunset when we collapse from exhaustion, desperately seeking rest. Grace

---

[17] (5 is numerically the value of grace!)

operates from a place of rest first. Instead of working to rest, grace rests so you can work. This is vital to understanding how the Kingdom operates in your life. You cannot bring Western processes into this Kingdom and expect them to produce. This is why the writer of the book of Hebrews says in the fourth chapter that there is still a rest for the people of God. They haven't yet understood they were created to operate from a place of rest.

THE SERIOUS SIDE TO THE GOOD OF GRACE

Let's continue on for one further look at this pattern of pleasure in the Genesis account.

> *And God said, Let there be a firmament in the midst of the waters, and let it divide the waters from the waters. (7) And God made the firmament, and divided the waters which were under the firmament from the waters which were above the firmament: and it was so. (8) And God called the firmament Heaven. And the evening and the morning were the second day. (9) And God said, Let the waters under the heaven be gathered together unto one place, and let the dry land appear: and it was so. (10) And God called the dry land Earth; and the gathering together of the waters called He Seas: and God saw that it was good. (11) And God said, Let the earth bring forth grass, the herb yielding seed, and the fruit tree yielding fruit after his kind, whose seed is in itself, upon the earth: and it was so. (12) And the earth brought forth grass, and herb yielding seed after his kind, and the tree yielding fruit, whose seed was in itself, after his kind: and God saw that it was good. (13) And the evening and the morning were the third day. (Genesis 1:6-13)*

These verses describe the next two days: The second day for the creation of the heavens and the third day for the creation of the seas, earth and the grasses. Using the same question, do you see where the pleasure of God is listed? (Hint: good) How often did this pleasure occur for the Father? Here comes the real question: On what day did this pleasure occur on?

If you've followed along with me so far, you've should have picked out the word *"good"* is found in verses 10 and 12. Both of these verses fall on the third day of creation and hold a special meaning for those who are Hebrew. If you were to look into the marriage records of the Hebrew population, you would discover the vast majority of these couples were married on the same day of the week – the third day – because of their belief there is a double blessing on this day by God. Anyone being married on this day, they believe, will receive the benefit of this blessing. Considering all the terms rolled into this blessing of *"good,"* it may well be something to keep in mind if you're of the marrying persuasion.

"But what about the second day?" you may be asking. I can't tell you why there wasn't anything good and pleasurable on that day. But I have my thoughts. Consider this for a moment: Our opening passage from Luke 12:32 said it was, *"...the Father's good pleasure to give you the kingdom."* I would conclude from this if something was not good for me, then He would not give it to me. So whatever was created on the second day is something I'm not supposed to have, or in Kingdom terms, I'm not supposed to have dominion over. What exactly did The Father keep from us on the second day? The Heavens – His domain.

Let me further this along a bit more. Again this is just my thought. If I'm not supposed to have dominion in the Heavens, then if I die and go to Heaven, I'm in a place which is not pleasing to the Father for me. Can it be that the Father gives us the gift of eternal life so we can be pleasing to Him from Earth? For on Earth we have been given dominion and authority – taking care of things! If you think this too far-fetched, read the last chapter of Revelation and see where all mankind ends up. But again, this is just my thought, right? (Not anymore.)

GOOD, LIKE GRACE, ABOUNDS

In the opening chapter of Genesis you will find there are no less than seven uses of the term *"good."* If you're into the number thing in scriptures this represents completeness. And what a way it was completed!

> *Then God saw everything that He had made, and indeed it was very good. So the evening and the morning were the sixth day. (Genesis 1:31)*

The word *"very"* in this passage carries in its interpretation a picture of a rake which vehemently stirs up the coals of a fire to keep them burning brightly so that you can stay warm. In six previous occasions the Father was pleased by the expression of His Word's work. When the last thing was created, and He looked over all He had done, He declared there was a pleasure which burned deep within Him for what He had just done. And what was the last thing which capped off His creation?

GOOD GIFTS

Before I jump into what happened in the creation events, I want to bring a further point out regarding *"goodness."* There are a couple of passages I want to bring to your attention.

> *Or do you despise the riches of His goodness, forbearance, and longsuffering, not knowing that the goodness of God leads you to repentance? (Romans 2:4)*

God's goodness leads us to repentance. I'm not going to get all religious here but do you understand by what it means to *"repent"*?

Religion has built up an edifice around this term which keeps people from its simple truth, and unfortunately keeps a great number of people from entering the Kingdom. Obviously, the term means to show sorrow for sins committed, but there is something more in the word that should be revealed.

I covered in great detail in my book *Eternal Life. Yes Forever!* that the suffix *"re"* has the meaning of returning back to the original condition or state of being. The word *"pent"* has a number of meanings in its usage, one being the high place as in the term *"penthouse"*, and another being the Greek term which represents the numeric value of five, a number Bible scholars all agree represents *"grace."* So repenting means more than acting in a sorrowful state about a sin: It holds in it the ability to return us back to our original high position of grace. Yet notice in this verse that only one thing leads us to this act of repenting – the goodness of God.

Now I want you to see something about this from the life of Moses. In Exodus 33, God has brought the children of Israel out of Egypt, and Moses has ascended up Mount Sinai for the second time. In this chapter Moses encounters something very unique about the nature of God as he confirms God will be with them as they proceed into the Promised Land.

> Then Moses said to the LORD, "See, You say to me, 'Bring up this people.' But You have not let me know whom You will send with me. Yet You have said, 'I know you by name, and you have also found grace in My sight.' (13) Now therefore, I pray, if I have found grace in Your sight, show me now Your way, that I may know You and that I may find grace in Your sight. And consider that this nation is Your people." (14) And He said, "My Presence will go with you, and I will give you rest." (15) Then he said to Him, "If Your Presence does not go with us, do not bring us up from here. (16) For how

then will it be known that Your people and I have found grace in Your sight, except You go with us? So we shall be separate, Your people and I, from all the people who are upon the face of the earth." (17) So the LORD said to Moses, "I will also do this thing that you have spoken; for you have found grace in My sight, and I know you by name." (18) And he said, "Please, show me Your glory." **(19) Then He said, "I will make all My goodness pass before you, and I will proclaim the name of the LORD before you. I will be gracious to whom I will be gracious, and I will have compassion on whom I will have compassion."** *(20) But He said, "You cannot see My face; for no man shall see Me, and live." (Exodus 33:12-20)*

I have stated before that the meaning of the Hebrew term for grace is different than the Greek term for grace. Without getting into too much detail, the difference which is quickest to convey has to do with posture: The Hebrew word depicts kneeling, while the Greek form expresses joy.

In this passage we see how Moses found grace in the sight of God; he then asks God to affirm that He will go with the children of Israel. After God acknowledges this request, what occurs next is baffling to most readers.

Moses asks to see the glory of God. He wants to see all of what defines the Kingdom of God. Recall how Moses, when he was in Egypt as member of Pharaoh's household, he was often in the glory display of a man's kingdom. His request here, in verse 18, was a natural response to see the abundance of a kingdom in order to assess the greatness of a king.

Don't assume for a moment here Moses is judging the Kingdom of God. When kings come in union with one another, it is common for each to display the abundance their realm contains. It is out of this abundance, gifts will be presented to one another, as a display of the *"grace"* of their kingdom. Moses' request here is really a request to understand the protocol of the Kingdom of God so he may be able to properly represent the children of Israel in the Kingdom of God.

However, notice what God's response to Moses is: *"I will make all My goodness pass before you."* This statement defines the ways of God. His goodness, not His Glory, is how the Kingdom is recognized and operates. It is not defined by all of its wealth of material items but by the nature of the King Himself.

What is important here is how God clearly demonstrates that the kingdom display of material objects does not make any reference to how those objects were obtained. Things can be given, bought, or stolen, yet once obtained, no one truly knows how they arrived, let alone how they have been retained. If we merely look upon things and say this is truly a king of many resources, we fail to know the true nature of the king and ultimately the kingdom itself. By clearly distinguishing that His kingdom comes out of His goodness, God has declared whatever *"things"* we see of Him, they all come from His nature of goodness. So as the book of James tells us, *"...every good and perfect gift comes from the Father..."* not as indication of His wealth, but out of His goodness towards us, a goodness which leads us back to the high place of grace.

Man's Purpose in Grace

Now that you better understand the nature of *"good"* as you look at the creation event and the seven references to the term *"good"* in Genesis 1, you should be able to recognize each daily event demonstrated not the capabilities of God merely to create, but represented His nature in how He created, and the pleasure He experienced as a result. In every occurrence when you read, *"...It was good..."* you encounter exactly what Moses experienced on the Mount as the goodness of God passed before him.

Understanding goodness also provides you with the ability to recognize when it is lacking. Did you know the creation event provides an example of this?

> *This is the history of the heavens and the earth when they were created, in the day that the LORD God made the earth and the heavens, (5) before any plant of the field was in the earth and before any herb of the field had grown. For the LORD God had not caused it to rain on the earth, and there was no man to till the ground; (6) but a mist went up from the earth and watered the whole face of the ground. (7) And the LORD God formed man of the dust of the ground, and breathed into his nostrils the breath of life; and man became a living being. (8) The LORD God planted a garden eastward in Eden, and there He put the man whom He had formed. (Genesis 2:4-8)*

Chapter 1 of Genesis describes the creation events from day one to six culminating with the proclamation that all God had created was *"very good."* The second chapter starts with God setting apart and blessing the seventh day as a day of rest for man. We pick up in verse 4 an expansion of the narrative of the sixth day, operating fully in the nature of grace, to see how things progressed towards this ultimate proclamation of, "...very good!" Verse 5 tells us the plants were waiting for the creation of man in order for them to begin to grow since the ground hadn't been tilled, even though it was being watered from the mist which was coming up out of the earth. In the seventh verse we discover how God formed man from the dust of the earth and breathed into his nostrils the breath of life.

The term *"formed"* in verse 7 describes a process similar to the manipulations which a potter performs when drawing out the desired form from a piece of clay through the use of pressure. Considering that man was created from the dust of the earth, this is an appropriate description of how God formed man. This is also the only indication in the creation where God used His hands to create an object. All other elements appear to be created from God's word or command. This distinction can't be stressed enough since God declared that man was to be like Him in image and likeness. All other items were dictated as to their purpose and existence, while man's distinct formation indicates the free will purpose which marks his existence.

> *Then the LORD God took the man and put him in the garden of Eden to tend and keep it. (16) And the LORD God commanded the man, saying, "Of every tree of the garden you may freely eat; (17) but of the tree of the knowledge of good and evil you shall not eat, for in the day that you eat of it you shall surely die." (18) And the LORD God said, "It is not good that man should be alone; I will make him a helper comparable to him." (19) Out of the ground the LORD God formed every beast of the field and every bird of the air, and brought them to Adam to see what he would call them. And whatever Adam called each living creature, that was its name. (20) So Adam gave names to all cattle, to the birds of the air, and to every beast of the field. But for Adam there was not found a helper comparable to him. (Genesis 2:15-20)*

We see previously in verse 8, after man became a living being, God placed him in a garden east of where he was formed. As ideal as the Garden of Eden was, man was not created in it; he shares none of the properties of that environment. In verse 15 we see the man is contracted to be there for God's purpose of tending and keeping it. If the man had been originally created in the garden, he would have immediate dominion over that area, and God would not be able to displace him from his *"domain"* except through battle. By placing the man in the garden, God is indicating that the tending and keeping of the garden created an expectation towards a moment of completion, or subjection for dominion to be conferred. Any failure in achieving this end would result in the delay of dominion. Every kingdom must be fought for to be awarded and retained. This is what Jesus meant when He said, *"...the kingdom of God suffers violence and the violent take it by force."*

So what does it mean that man was placed in the garden to *"tend and keep it?"* The words "tend" and "keep" have separate and very distinct meaning to the purpose the man was to fulfill. The Hebraic meaning of the word recorded as *"tend"* carries the meaning to till the ground as a husbandman or laborer.

Much of society has lost its understanding of tilling as we have moved away from an agricultural social order towards a specialized, industrial social order. We miss the nature of tilling to turn over and expose hidden matter; of the preparation of the soil to receive the seed; of the focus of keeping weeds from overtaking the crop; and of feeding the soil the nutrients required to promote the growth of the seed.

This same word also is used to describe a servant and worshiper. So we see here how man's job to till the garden was to uncover hidden things while preparing a place for the seed to be implanted and nourished. This activity acted as a service of worship towards God.

The Hebrew word for *"keep"* in this passage means to be a watchman, or a guard who watches with a very narrow, intent gaze. It implies that the person is responsible for overseeing the life of the garden by restraining any invading force. We see therefore two functions man was to perform while employed in the garden: Worshipful service to the seed of God's creative word and protector of the environment which the seed was to produce its fruit in.

In verses 16 and 17 we see the contract restriction to man's employment with God in the garden. It clearly defines all of the work being performed in the garden had a limit upon man's ability to enjoy all the rewards from those efforts.

God's Gift to Man

But as great as the garden is, please understand this was not a gift to man. It was man's work, duty, or service. Today we often make the mistake of thanking God for the gift of our work. I'm not saying we shouldn't thank God for work, but our employment, whatever it may be, is not a gift from the grace realm. It is a function of our responsibility to till.

Yes, I realize some of you may disagree with me about this but consider this. Proverbs 10:22 tells us the blessing of the Lord, while making you rich, does not add sorrow to it. A job, while it can make you rich, it also will add sorrow. If every good and perfect gift comes from the Father, contained in the gift is the blessing of the Father. This blessing activates the abundant nature of grace in the gift making it a life-giving property to all who come in contact with it. If you claim God blessed you with a job as a gift of His grace, I simply have to ask you if the gift is giving life to all who come in contact with it; and will this principle continue to operate if you're not involved in it. Employment is our worship to God where we demonstrate the nature of His Kingdom to those who do not know Him.

Returning to our man in the garden, verse 18 must stand out in this study, as well as any other study of God's handiwork. In this verse we hear God declare that something isn't good, meaning it lacks the pleasure associated with the Kingdom of Grace. Notice God is declaring this about man, not about God's Kingdom. Man was created to be in the likeness and image of God and yet God declares how man being alone is not good, or doesn't align with the principle of a

Kingdom of Grace. Throughout the entire creation event we have seen *"goodness"* was God's final declaration, yet man's existence is deemed *"not good"* if he is alone. Another way of saying this is, the pleasure of grace is not complete in the life of man when there is no one to give to.

God's decree of *"not good"* also contains within it the answer which will correct the matter and bring it to completion. God will make a helper comparable to the man. But look what follows. Adam names the animals. No helper, just name the animals. What gives here? This is one of the examples of the ways of God.

As I stated a moment ago, God declared it was not good for man to be alone. Man did not make this observation, God did. Man didn't yet know there was something amiss. The Hebrew teachers say the reason God had Adam name the animals first was so that he could see for himself there was something different between the pairings of the animals, with the commission which God had placed upon them to be fruitful and multiply, and himself with the same commission. Only after he had completed this task could Adam fully recognize and understand how he did not have a partner to fulfill his commission. We often are called to perform a task for God's kingdom not recognizing that what we discover in our performance is the missing element in us fulfilling our commission.

> *And the LORD God caused a deep sleep to fall on Adam, and he slept; and He took one of his ribs, and closed up the flesh in its place. (22) Then the rib which the LORD God had taken from man He made into a woman, and He brought her to the man. (23) And Adam said: "This is now bone of my bones And flesh of my flesh; She shall be called Woman, Because she was taken out of Man." (Genesis 2:21-23)*

In the creation event we see the workings of abounding grace in how everything which is made comes from the environment it resides and abounds in: Stars made from the elements of space; birds from the elements of the sky; fish from the elements of the water; and beasts from the elements of the earth. Man too is made from the earth, yet different from the animals since God formed him and breathed life into his body. His body abounds upon the earth while his spirit abounds in the eternal realm. But now we see the last creation act of God making a woman out of an element of man. This element, the rib, tells us the woman is to abound at the side of man, not at his foot, his head or his backside.

An important aspect of grace many overlook has to do with honor. This honor is evident in the Kingdom by the presence of the throne of grace. As grace operated in the creation event, the highest honor is given to each object which reflects the fullness of the elements it came from. Man received the highest honor being the fullness of not only the dust of the earth but the image of God also. In this same manner, the woman receives the highest honor being made from man. This is not an honor of authority over man but honor as a crown upon man.

In verse 22 we find something unique about this creative act. Here we find God *"made"* the woman. This word is entirely different from the word which described how God formed man. This word conveys the picture of God going away to a place to design and fashion the woman with serious intent. Upon the completion of this creative act, we are told God *"brought"* her to the man. The word *"brought"* portrays the act of giving or setting down. In this verse we witness the goodness and grace of the King giving a *"crown"* as a *"gift"* to the man. Said another way, the woman is the first grace-gift to man. Yes, despite what you may feel or have heard in the past, *a woman is a gift from God to man purposely designed and fashioned to work alongside and provide honor to man.*

It might be best if you stop here for a moment. This last statement needs to be fully ingested before you go forward, since what I'm about to say next is entirely dependent upon your understanding this truth.

Several thousand years after God brought the woman to Adam, the Apostle Paul tells the church of Ephesus that the response which Adam made about his gift from God, is exactly the same in character to how Christ views the church. And despite all Paul knew about *charis*, he claimed that this relationship is a great mystery! The grace-gift of the church to Christ is still being revealed on Earth. But just how is this being done?

BEING GRACE

> *As every man hath received the **gift**, even so minister the same one to another, as good stewards of the manifold grace of God. (1 Peter 4:10)*

You are a steward of God's grace. Do you realize this? This isn't something which will someday happen to you. It is going on right this moment. It has been a reality since the creation of man. What Adam lost in the garden has been regained at the resurrection of Jesus.

Look carefully at the wording in this verse and follow the pattern according to what you have learned. 1. A gift was given and received; 2. The gift is now to be given to another; 3. The release of the gift demonstrates the varied nature of God's grace. At no point in this transaction is the gift held onto. In order for it to be a demonstration of grace it must be released. You are deemed a good steward when the full transaction is completed.

Action. This is the characteristic of a verb. I know I'm repeating myself here but I need to make this point clear. In this verse the word *"gift"* is a *charis* word. More importantly, its Greek root word is the verb-tense of *charis*. Even more important than the last statement is how this single word has been demonized in all religious circles. As such, I am deciding not to reveal it at this time so you may not put your spiritual blinders on before I get finished.

The title of this section is not *"Doing Grace"* which some of you might feel would be appropriate if I'm going to speak about the action of grace. However, this would imply that by doing, you could also choose not to do. Worded in another manner, you could choose to not do the will of the Father! Does this sound like the actions of a good steward?

Ponder this: Did you teach your pet dog to bark or pet cat to meow? Why not? Obviously, you don't have to do this because it is a feature which is *"built in"* to the model of pet you have. They do this because of how they are made. Or, out of their being they do these things naturally. Your ability to control, or limit, the use of this feature is what classifies you as a good owner, or steward, of your pet in the eyes of the public. Now granted, not everyone likes pets; so despite what you may think about them being a gift, their nature can offend.

For those of you who may at this point become slow of thought, let me apply this example to you. Your old nature was not a gift given to mankind from God. Because of your old nature, you did things which offended God. Even those things which you thought were *"good"* were offensive to God.

The Father knew your past actions were a result of the stewardship you were under; however, those actions were based on a corrupted nature. In His infinite wisdom, Father gives you a glimpse of His goodness. Desiring to receive more of this goodness, you believe in His

Son's works and the Father births a new nature in you. Next, He places you under the stewardship of Holy Spirit so you can learn how to properly give the gift of this new nature He placed within you.

It is from *"being"* the new nature where you *"do"* the acts people recognize as grace. Everything you henceforth do, from the smallest to the most monumental, comes from being. All that you do is evidence of the grace-gift you have received and give away to those around you. Notice how the grace-gift is not for you, but for those around you. The grace-gift you require, conversely, is in someone else who you need to locate, or who is searching for you.

Before I move further, let me nip something which may be circulating in the back of your mind. *"Be good."* Have you ever heard this, or told someone to act this way? Do you recall what exactly you were supposed to do to *"be good?"* Remember, *"good"* represents the pleasure of an act of God's creative purpose. Many people are trying to get to a state of *"being"* by doing, or not doing, acts which appear *"good."* These are the actions of the fallen nature. If God has already decreed that something is *"good,"* why are we trying to redefine its nature with a man-made rendition which doesn't have any pleasure associated with it?

THE ACTS OF BEING

> *Now there are diversities of **gifts**, but the same Spirit. (1 Corinthians 12:4)*

Have you ever met someone and they seem to have it all together? Everything comes their way. There is not a situation where they are even a bit ruffled. You just stand and look at them in awe of what occurs around, and through them. If there is one word which describes how these people operate, it has to be the word from this verse: they are "gifted."

Now I know what some of you might be thinking, *"This isn't a verse for them. They aren't saved!"*

> For the **gifts** and calling of God are without repentance.
> *(Romans 11:29)*

This word, gifts, as I've said, has been demonized by the religious circles. It is the Greek word, *charisma*. Consider how the world equates this word with sex appeal, charm, mystique, personality, glamour and magnetism. You know, all the traits which are birthed in an inflated ego. It is the antithesis of the holiness all religion extols.

However, this is a "grace word" and is a gifting from God which He won't repent giving! Is it possible Jesus demonstrated these very same attributes in a fashion which aligned with the Kingdom of Heaven and mankind? If we are told Jesus grew in grace and wisdom with God and man, is it possible the grace He grew in was a reflection of the *charisma*, or grace gift, God placed within him? How else could you explain the swarms of people who gathered around Him? It wasn't because He was a geek or some weirdo. He had a gift, people recognized it, and they wanted to be around it simply because it made them feel *"good."*

Please, for a moment, step away from the backwaters of the religious bile which has been pumped into you. I want you to understand this one thing: God has placed within you a gift, a gifting, which flows easily from your being. You don't have to work at it, it comes naturally. When you are operating in your gifting, all time stands still as you work for the eternal purpose residing within you. People are drawn to your gifting just as moths are drawn to a light.

This gifting is your grace-gift to the world which demonstrates the manifold grace of God. When you hide it, or cloak it in veiled humility, you are not being the good steward God expects you to be of the gift He gave you.

I want you to consider the gifting of the Olympic champion Usain Bolt, who many consider to be the fastest man in the world. His bravado on the field has earned him a reputation of being arrogant. However, the demonstration of his ability continually defies and amazes his critics. Why shouldn't we all celebrate the grace-gift God has placed within this man and encourage him to excel in his chosen field?

It is possible I just pricked something in you which you never considered. Every gifting we all display and operate in is a direct gift of grace from the Father. As such, it should be honored, and celebrated, as a holy endowment purposed for our *"pleasure."* I know this kind of statement can get weird and blow up in a whole lot of different directions, so I'm not going to take it any further than this. My point is to get you to think beyond the religious box of grace and look at the purposes of the Kingdom.

When was the last time you heard a friend or co-worker extol the virtues of a really great sermon given by your pastor from a year ago? However, they'll all remark about how effortlessly and graceful Usain Bolt ran in every 200 meters event he has participated in over the last four years. If both of these men are operating from the fullness of their grace-gift, how can one be better than the other? Religion will try to make a comparison in order to justify its base of power. However, in the Kingdom, their ability is merely a reflection of the grace God has purposed for this time. The gifts of both hold equal value in the Kingdom of God.

"But how can that be possible? A track star can't be as important as a pastor!" is what I'm hearing. This comment reflects the world's influence which you have allowed to dictate how you relate to people.

How about I put it this way: a pastor and a garbage collector both have equal value in the Kingdom of God. Before you give me the same response, realize how far you've drifted. The gift given by the Father and demonstrated in the person is what is valuable.

Jesus, our brother, stated that He and the Father are one. His desire in John 17 was that we would be one with them. This is not one-plus or one-minus: it is just one. All our gifts, or grace, come from Him, not to lift us up, but to lift Him up so all men will be drawn to Him. This is our role of being *"...in Him."* How else do you think you're going to do greater works than Jesus?

Don't pull the humble pie routine here. *"I can never do greater works than Jesus."* This statement, and the spirit behind it, is the most prideful thing you could ever say. Jesus said we would do greater works and then went to the cross for all of us. This statement means that what He did wasn't enough for you to complete what He said! What about *"...it is finished!"* don't you understand?

All right, just admit it - you're afraid. You're scared. WRONG! God has not given you the spirit of fear but of power, love, and a sound mind. Greater is He that lives in you than he who lives in the world! If God be for you, who can be against you? With man it is impossible, but with God all things are possible. (I could go on, but I hope you get the point.)

> *A man's gift maketh room for him, and bringeth him before great men. (Proverbs 18:16)*

You have a purpose, a plan and a destiny to fulfill which the Father prepared in the very word that birthed you. To accomplish this, He gave you a gift only you possess; no one else. It is specifically designed to operate in you at its fullest potential. When you employ it, you will be recognized as having *"charisma."* The question you have to answer is: Can you be, and do, what you have been prepared to do?

Many will answer this question, *"Only if God gives me the grace to do it."* This statement, and its variation, *"God give me more grace,"* is heresy in a Kingdom of grace. How is it possible for there to be a lack of grace in your life? Does not grace much more abound? Furthermore, doesn't John 1:16 say that we received the fullness of grace in Jesus? If we're in Him, how can you express a need for something that is already full and abounding?

Let me answer this dilemma with an example. Have you ever seen those little Russian dolls that are stacked within each other? A larger doll opens up to reveal another doll painted to look just like the outer doll. This inner doll conversely houses a smaller version of the same doll, so on and so on until you get to a very small doll in the very center. Each doll is painted exactly the same so that there is no visual difference other than size.

What I have just described is the grace-gift you possess. From all outward appearances it is singular in nature which creates the perception that more grace is needed. What we don't realize is that the Father really loves to give gifts which cause us to dig deeper. Most fail to understand how there is abundance within their gift which waits to be revealed. You don't need more – you need to continually unveil the depths and levels of the grace placed within you.

A steward of the manifold grace of God does not sit on one gift thinking this is all I've got. They understand how they have a position of managing variety and one gift does not variety make. The cry of "more" is a siren warning you of the lack of knowing the abundance which has been placed within you which is seeking to be unveiled. If you're going to "be" in this Kingdom so that you can "do" the good works, grace demands your involvement in discovering the fullness placed within you. The days have passed where we can merely claimed, "I'm saved by grace," and not advance into the depth of positions we have been destined for.

REIGNING IN GRACE

Back in the chapter "The Pleasure of Grace" I brought up the matter of grace reigns through righteousness. This was in reference to a passage out of Romans 5.

> *Moreover the law entered, that the offence might abound. But where sin abounded, grace did much more abound: (21) That as sin hath reigned unto death, even so might* **grace reign through righteousness** *unto eternal life by Jesus Christ our Lord. (Romans 5:20-21)*

"Reigning" is a term which deals with dominion, power and authority. This is the original intent of the Father for all of His children on this planet. Notice that in order for grace to properly have dominion, power and authority it must be conducted through righteousness. This righteousness we have received from Jesus Christ is so our grace can function in the manner of the Kingdom of Grace. Your grace-gift, through Jesus, is designed to exhibit dominion, power and authority.

However, gifts have been given which are not operating according to their original intent. These gifts, nonetheless, still exhibit the design – their dominion, power and authority are just directed towards death.

I stated earlier that in the Greek and Roman cultures, one of the ways in which a person advanced in their station in life was to seek out the *charis,* or favor, of a benefactor. Often these favors came with a price which the person was expected to pay to move into the public office. Paul, in this passage in Romans 5, just as he did in Ephesians

2:9, demonstrates how a relationship with, and through, Christ is the only acceptable way a grace-gift can produce according to the Kingdom principle of abounding life.

What does this mean to you? You have to recognize that every person around you has a unique grace-gifting. It is a reflection of the manifold grace of God in their life. However, is it producing the evidence of eternal life, or death? The world will use a gifting to the bitter end and then look for another to fill the spot left vacant. The Kingdom will display it forever, simply because the gift continually glorifies God. So ask yourself, "Is my grace-gift creating life or preventing life from thriving?"

There is a clarification at this point which I must make: Your talent is not your grace-gift. I know how many a preacher has attached the parable of the unjust servant who buried his talent instead of putting it in the bank to earn interest as a vehicle to get people to use the gift God placed inside of them. But they are not complete in their thinking about the matter. How could I make such a claim?

Consider how the Father buried a gifting in you in order for you to till the soil (what you're made of) and find the treasure (what He looks like in you). This was the purpose for Adam in the Garden, just as it is your purpose today. Many don't even know they are expected to find this treasure in themselves. They just assume because they have a proficiency, or talent, in a particular area, this is their gifting. Your grace-gift will work through your talent, but they are not one in the same thing.

If you have difficulty understanding this, consider someone who is athletic. They may run faster, jump higher, throw further, or endure longer as an expression of their talent. But if they become injured and are unable to compete, would this indicate that their grace-gift is ended also? Obviously not, since only the ability to express their talent is hampered.

I can't stress the importance of this enough since many congregants are subjecting themselves to "spiritual gifting" tests in order to determine what their "gift" is for the "body" they are in. Most of these tests rely on what are the talents you have developed in the "world" prior to salvation and continue to operate in. Some "spiritual" title is then attached to "your gift" so you can attend to the parking lot ministry for the house. If this has happened to you, consider what would happen if you suddenly lost your eyesight. Would the leadership tell you that your gift suddenly didn't fit the needs of the house, or parking lot ministry? As in the example of the athlete, only the talent has been affected – not the grace-gift given by the Father.

Being ambassadors for the Kingdom of God places within our hands the responsibility of presenting to the world an example of who the Father is. His faith in us to use the giftings He gave to each one of us assures us that whatever we do to bring Heaven on Earth, it will please Him. So are you ready to give your grace to someone just like Jesus did?

Epilogue

Throughout this manuscript I have tried to show you how grace viewed from the perspective of the Kingdom of God has a multitude of characteristics which most are not even aware of. I have intentionally stayed away from the formal traditions of looking at this subject under the guise of divine grace versus common grace simply because too many have already plowed that field. There is nothing wrong with their approach if you are only going to view the matter of grace from the fallen nature. My quest has been to provide a thought about what is the original intention of the acts of grace and what is to happen with the expression of this grace after your salvation experience.

The need to look into your future according to the intent of the Father is something lacking in many congregations. The franchise, seeker-friendly, mega-church mentality on one end of the spectrum and "my four and no one more" at the other end are stifling environments which keep congregants from discovering how God gifted them. Completing a "spiritual gifts" assessment in order to determine how members fit in the operation of the "house" does not explain or expand what their Kingdom purpose is either.

Since every believer is called to be leaders, ask yourself these questions about your grace gift.

- Is my gifting producing joy not only in myself but those around me?

- Is there a demonstration of reciprocal giving when I'm in my gifting?

- Can *"thankfulness"* properly describe the outcome of my grace-gift?

- Is my grace-gift creating an environment of honor through accessing the gift in others?

- Are those closest to me aware of the grace-gift I function in or has it become *"natural"* in their eyes?

Charis, gratia, or *grace* is an expanding topic which one book cannot hope to encompass. I would encourage you to begin your own study on this important part of your spiritual identity. Pass along your insights to those who have been entrusted to you so they too may grow into the plans and purposes the Father has prepared for them.

At the start of this book I had you take all the representations of how or what you knew grace to be and place them into a wagon. Now, if you wish, take them out and examine them. In this new light of revelation they are still valid, yet their allure may have dimmed in the light of the true jewel of grace as seen from the Kingdom of God.

My claim in the beginning was to move you into an understanding of grace from the Kingdom of God using Hebrews 4:16 as the backdrop.

> *Let us therefore come boldly unto the throne of grace, that we may obtain mercy, and find grace to help in time of need. (Hebrews 4:16)*

After reading this material, what do you now understand about:

1. Coming boldly to a throne;

2. The meaning of a throne of grace;

3. Obtaining mercy at the throne;

4. Finding grace to help;

5. Grace in a time of need.

Thank you for taking the time to explore this matter in a graceful fashion. You are more than welcome to send me any insights you feel might further this dialogue along. My hope is that you can now see how your life has a greater purpose than just being *"a sinner saved by grace."*

Charis, *chesed*, and *shalom* to you

Mike

Appendix I

THE WORD OF GRACE

In this study it would assist us to know what the *"grace"* words are as I have indicated throughout the text. For our purposes here, a *"grace"* word is any word which has the Strong's Greek numeric value 5485 as a root word for part of its definition. The following are those words, their definition as recorded in Strong's Concordance, with their corresponding number. Additionally, since the root meaning is so vital in understanding a word, I have included the root word for grace also. I trust you'll be able to use this as a reference in this study.

Strong's #	Greek Word	Strong's Definition
G5463	Chairō	A primary verb; to be full of "cheer", that is, calmly happy or well off; impersonal especially as a salutation (on meeting or parting), be well: – farewell, be glad, God speed, greeting, hail, joy (-fully), rejoice.
G5485	*Charis*	From G5463; graciousness (as gratifying), of manner or act (abstract or concrete; literal, figurative or spiritual; especially the divine influence upon the heart, and its reflection in the life; including gratitude): – acceptable, benefit, favour, gift, grace (-ious),

Strong's #	Greek Word	Strong's Definition
		joy liberality, pleasure, thank (-s, -worthy).
G5483	Charizomai	Middle voice from G5485; to grant as a favor, that is, gratuitously, in kindness, pardon or rescue: – deliver, (frankly) forgive, (freely) give, grant.
G5484	Charin	Accusative case of G5485 as preposition; through favor of, that is, on account of: – be- (for) cause of, for sake of, +... fore, X reproachfully.
G5487	Charitoō	From G5485; to grace, that is, indue with special honor: – make accepted, be highly favoured.

A DEEPER LOOK

With these basic *"grace"* words we now have a foundation to work from. There is also a series of words that have G5483, Charizomai, as their root word, further adding to the richness of our study.

Strong's #	Greek Word	Strong's Definition
G884	Acharistos	From G1 (as a negative particle) and a presumed derivative of G5483; thankless, that is, ungrateful: – unthankful.
G2168	Eucharisteō	From G2170; to be grateful, that is, (actually) to express gratitude (towards); specifically to say grace at a meal: – (give) thank (-ful, -s).
G2169	Eucharistia	From G2170; gratitude; actually grateful language (to God, as an act of worship): – thankfulness,

		(giving of) thanks (-giving).
G2170	Eucharistos	From G2095 and a derivative of G5483; well favored, that is, (by implication) grateful: – thankful.
G5486	Charisma	From G5483; a (divine) gratuity, that is, deliverance (from danger or passion); (specifically) a (spiritual) endowment, that is, (subjectively) religious qualification, or (objectively) miraculous faculty: – (free) gift.

Space does not permit me the opportunity to list each individual occurrence for every word where it appears in scripture. Yet I trust you will by knowing the definitions of these few words be able to recognize their use in the scriptures when you come across them. A bit of research from a Strong's Concordance is all that will be required to determine if it is one of these words.

Appendix II

GRATITUDE

One final thought. For all that I've unveiled or reiterated about the nature of grace, there is one thing I want to impart to you. Grace, while being a verb, is really an action precipitated from a thought – no an attitude. Grace is gratitude. If you're not grateful then don't try to fake it. We all know when this is happening.

Are you grateful for the sleep you've had; for the bed you've laid in; the smile of neighbor or a stranger; the way the sun breaks through the clouds and splashed across your face; the clothing which you've disguised your true essence with to meet the challenges of the day; your children, your parents, your friends, your pets, your lover; the way your hand lays in the hand of another; the wisps of hair that tickle your nose in the breeze; the smell of coffee on a cold morning; the sound of rush hour traffic; the thrill of staring into the eyes of your grandchild and seeing your youth; the smell of lilacs wafting into your cubical from the co-worker across the aisle; the press of the subway coming to your stop; the unsuppressed yawn of a three-year old in a public meeting; the smell of fresh cut lawn; or, how about you name something? There is much to be grateful for every moment of every day. All of it is a gift from grace to you.

In 1902, William George Jordan wrote a book entitled *The Power of Truth; Individual Problems and Possibilities.* Contained within that book is the following chapter which I have placed here to demonstrate the heart of grace.

"The Courage to Face Ingratitude"

By William George Jordan

INGRATITUDE, the most popular sin of humanity, is forgetfulness of the heart. It is the revelation of the emptiness of pretended loyalty. The individual who possesses it finds it the shortest cut to all the other vices.

Ingratitude is a crime more despicable than revenge, which is only returning evil for evil, while ingratitude returns evil for good...

Gratitude is thankfulness expressed in action. It is the instinctive radiation of justice, giving new life and energy to the individual from whom it emanates. It is the heart's recognition of kindness that the lips cannot repay. Gratitude never counts its payments. It realizes that no debt of kindness can ever be outlawed, ever be cancelled, ever paid in full. Gratitude ever feels the insignificance of its installments; ingratitude the nothingness of the debt. Gratitude is the flowering of a seed of kindness; ingratitude is the dead inactivity of a seed dropped on a stone.

The expectation of gratitude is human; the rising superior to ingratitude is almost divine. To desire recognition of our acts of kindness and to hunger for appreciation and the simple justice of a return of good for good, is natural. But man never rises to the dignity of true living until he has the courage that dares to face ingratitude calmly, and to pursue his course unchanged when his good works meet with thanklessness or disdain. Man should have only one court of appeals as to his actions, not "what will be the result?" "how will it be received?" but "is it right?" Then he should live his life in harmony with this standard alone, serenely, bravely, loyally and unfalteringly, making "right for right's sake" both his ideal and his inspiration. Man should not be an automatic gas-machine, cleverly contrived to release a given quantity of illumination under the stimulus of a nickel. He should be like the great sun itself which ever radiates light, warmth, life and power, because it cannot help doing so, because these qualities fill the heart of the sun, and for it to have them means that it must give them constantly. Let the sunlight of our sympathy, tenderness, love, appreciation, influence and kindness ever go out from us as a glow to brighten and hearten others. But do not let us ever spoil it all by going through life constantly collecting receipts, as vouchers, to stick on the file of our self-approval.

It is hard to see those who have sat at our board in the days of our prosperity, flee as from a pestilence when misfortune darkens our doorway; to see the loyalty upon which we would have staked our life, that seemed firm as a rock, crack and splinter like thin glass at the first real test; to know that the fire of friendship at which we could ever warm our hands in our hour of need, has turned to cold, dead, gray ashes, where warmth is but a haunting memory.

To realize that he who once lived in the sanctuary of our affection, in the frank confidence where conversation seemed but our soliloquy, and to whom our aims and aspirations have been thrown open with no Bluebeard chamber of reserve, has been secretly poisoning the waters of our reputation and undermining us by his lies and treachery, is hard indeed. But no matter how the ingratitude stings us, we should just swallow the sob, stifle the tear, smile serenely and bravely, and— seek to forget.

In justice to ourselves we should not permit the ingratitude of a few to make us condemn the whole world. We pay too much tribute to a few human insects when we let their wrong-doing paralyze our faith in humanity. It is a lie of the cynics that says "all men are ungrateful," a companion lie to "all men have their price." We must trust humanity if we would get good from humanity. He who thinks all mankind is vile is a pessimist who mistakes his introspection for observation; he looks into his own heart and thinks he sees the world. He is like a cross-eyed man, who never sees what he seems to be looking at. Confidence and credit are the cornerstones of business, as they are of society. Withdraw them from business and the activities and enterprises of the world would stop in an instant, topple and fall into chaos. Withdraw confidence in humanity from the individual, and he becomes but a breathing, selfish egotist, the one good man left, working overtime in nursing his petty grudge against the world because a few whom he has favored have been ungrateful.

If a man receives a counterfeit dollar he does not straightway lose his faith in all money—at least there are no such instances on record in this country. If he has a run of three or four days of dull weather he does not say "the sun ceases to exist, there are surely no bright days to come in the whole calendar of time." If a man's breakfast is rendered an unpleasant memory by some item of food that has outlived its usefulness, he does not forswear eating. If a man finds under a tree an apple with a suspicious looking hole on one side, he does not condemn the whole orchard; he simply confines his criticism to that apple. But he who has helped someone who, later, did not pass a good examination on gratitude, says in a voice plaintive with the consciousness of injury, and with a nod of his head that implies the wisdom of Solomon: "I have had my experience, I have learned my lesson. This is the last time I will have faith in any man. I did this for him, and that for him, and now, look at the result!"

Then he unrolls a long schedule of favors, carefully itemized and added up, till it seems the payroll of a great city. He complains of the injustice of one man, yet he is willing to be unjust to the whole world, making it bear the punishment of the wrong of an individual. There is too much vicarious suffering already in this earth of ours without this lilliputian attempt to extend it by syndicating one man's ingratitude. If one man drinks to excess, it is not absolute justice to send the whole world to jail. The farmer does not expect every seed that he sows in hope and faith to fall on good ground and bring forth its harvest; he is perfectly certain that this will not be so, cannot be. He is counting on the final outcome of many seeds, on the harvest of all, rather than on the harvest of one...The more unselfish, charitable and exalted the life and mission of the individual, the larger will be the number of instances of ingratitude that must be met and vanquished...

We must ever tower high above dependence on human gratitude or we can do nothing really great, nothing truly noble. The expectation of gratitude is the alloy of an otherwise virtuous act. It ever dulls the edge of even our best actions. Most persons look at gratitude as a protective tariff on virtues. The man who is weakened in well-doing by the ingratitude of others, is serving God on a salary basis. He is a hired soldier, not a volunteer. He should be honest enough to see that he is working for a reward; like a child, he is being good for a bonus. He is really regarding his kindness and his other expressions of goodness as moral stock he is willing to hold only so long as they pay dividends. There is in such living always a touch of the pose; it is waiting for the applause of the gallery. We must let the consciousness of doing right, of living up to our ideals, be our reward and stimulus, or life will become to us but a series of failures, sorrows and disappointments...

Let us forget the good deeds we have done by making them seem small in comparison with the greater things we are doing, and the still greater acts we hope to do. This is true generosity, and will develop gratitude in the soul of him who has been helped, unless he is so petrified in selfishness as to make it impossible. But constantly reminding a man of the favors he has received from you almost cancels the debt. The care of the statistics should be his privilege; you are usurping his prerogative when you recall them. Merely because it has been our good fortune to be able to serve someone, we should not act as if we held a mortgage on his immortality, and expect him to swing the censer of adulation forever in our presence...

No good act performed in the world ever dies. Science tells us that no atom of matter can ever be destroyed, that no force once started ever ends; it merely passes through a multiplicity of ever-changing phases. Every good deed done to others is a great force that starts an unending pulsation through time and eternity. We may not know it, we may never hear a word of gratitude or of recognition, but it will all come back to us in some form as naturally, as perfectly, as inevitably, as echo answers to sound. Perhaps not as we expect it, how we expect it, nor where, but sometime, somehow, somewhere, it comes back, as the dove that Noah sent from the Ark returned with its green leaf of revelation. Let us conceive of gratitude in its largest, most beautiful sense, that if we receive any kindness we are debtor, not merely to one man, but to the whole world. As we are each day indebted to thousands for the comforts, joys, consolations, and blessings of life, let us realize that it is only by kindness to all that we can begin to repay the debt to one, begin to make gratitude the atmosphere of all our living and a constant expression in outward acts, rather than in mere thoughts. Let us see the awful cowardice and the injustice of ingratitude, not to take it too seriously in others, not to condemn it too severely, but merely to banish it forever from our own lives, and to make every hour of our living the radiation of the sweetness of gratitude.

Considering the nature of grace from the Kingdom, this glimpse at the affects of not being in grace rather aptly portrays the manners of a world which longs for us to demonstrate the empowering gift God has placed with us.

About the Author

Mike and his family live in Portland, Oregon, where he is one of the teachers of the Word of God at a local fellowship. As a graduate of the Latin University of Theology, Mike is passionate about people understanding what the Kingdom of God is, its impact in their lives and how it changes communities who are determined to operate from its authority.

Mike is the author of *Grace for Shame, Chesed: Beyond the Veil of Mercy, Your Life is a Freaking Mess and You Want Answers, A Kingdom Primer,* and *Eternal Life. Yes Forever!* Mike contributes his insights about the Kingdom of grace at www.graceforshame.com and www.mygrace2u.com.

Mike can be contacted at mike@mikehillebrecht.com

Additional titles by mike hillebrecht

Chesed
Beyond the Veil of Mercy

mike hillebrecht

What if what you knew from scriptures about mercy wasn't quite accurate? What if the blessings that we've been searching for have been locked away all this time in a simple Hebrew word that scholars agree has no English translation?

In this brief expose, teacher and author Mike Hillebrecht (Grace for Shame) explores the meaning of a Hebrew term that the original Bible scholars may have interpreted inaccurately into the Greek word we know as 'mercy. "You will begin to see how many of the Old and New Testament passages take on an entirely different meaning by understanding this key Hebrew word in its proper context.

Mike will take you through a practical explanation of the full meaning of coming to the throne of grace in God's Kingdom not with the expectation of judgment but with the fullest measure of equality. This is an eye-opening study that will impact your walk with the Lord and those that are around you.

ISBN/EAN13: 0615617352 / 9780615617350

Page Count: 70

Trim Size: 6″x 9″

Language: English

Color: Black and White

Related Categories: Religion / Biblical Studies / General

www.beyondthemercyveil.com

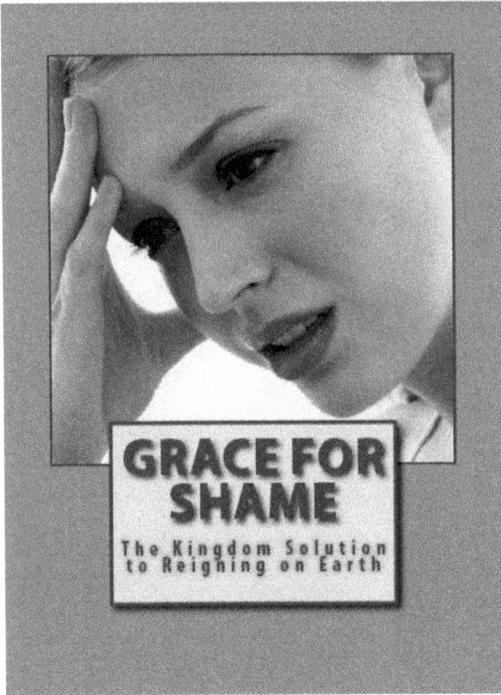

Shame. Embarrassment. Humiliation. The ugly trio. Their distinct occupation is to keep you seeing yourself as a sinner saved by grace rather than as a son seated next to the throne of grace. The distinction is about whether you are being reigned over or whether you're reigning. It's a battle for your predestined role in the Kingdom of God.

Inside *Grace for Shame* you will discover a fresh look at what grace truly looks like and how God designed it to operate in your life. This ain't your papa or mama's grace - this is grace straight from the Kingdom of God as it has been operating throughout all of eternity. You will find the grace that is intended to break off the shackles that the ugly trio has bound you with, imprisoning you from your destiny.

Expect to finally identify with the true kingdom meaning of the cross - not the sanitized message that religion has produced. Are you considered a prodigal son, or know someone who is? *Grace for Shame* gives a perspective from the Kingdom of God that it's not about your past but about how truly great you are right now in the eyes of the Father.

ISBN/EAN13: 0615605508 / 9780615605500

Page Count: 220

Trim Size: 6 ″x 9 ″

Language: English

Color: Black and White

Related Categories: Religion / Christian Life / Personal Growth

www.graceforshame.com

If you desire to be known as a Son of God according to Romans 8, you had better know the 3-R's of the Kingdom. They are the foundational tenets of the kingdom's interaction with you as a son. The Holy Spirit will not advance you to the head of the class if you miss any one of the important lessons these have to demonstrate. Within this booklet you will find covered the following items:

A KINGDOM PRIMER

THE BASICS OF THE KINGDOM OF GOD

MIKE HILLEBRECHT

The Father's intent – What was the original intent of God and how it changed.
Reconciliation – The Father's plan.
Redemption – The purpose of Jesus
Righteousness – The effect of reconciliation and redemption.
Right of Law – Where you are in God's time-line.
Royal Law – This is the one law given by the King.
Perfect Law – This is what we're striving to adhere too.
Peace – It may not be what you think.

As with the purpose of any primer, the entire spectrum of the topics offered cannot be presented to their fullest measure. This book is designed simply to be a building block which will provoke your thoughts about the matters at hand and spur you to search out further how they impact your walk with the Father.

ISBN/EAN13: 061562099X / 978-0615620992

Page Count: 126 pages

Trim Size: 6" x 9"

Language: English

Color: Black & White on White paper

Related Categories Religion / Biblical Studies / General

www.kingdomprimer.com

Live and not die! This is not the motto of some whacked out group of mercenaries. It belongs to a select group of people who believe that what Jesus Christ accomplished at the cross is supposed to be the norm for their lives.

What do you mean, "Thank goodness this isn't for me?"

Eternal life. Yes, Forever! is a stark look at a truth that has been turned sideways. Contained within, you will finally find the truth about the purpose of Heaven and how you're not supposed to go there except for dinner. Being "born again" versus being "saved" will be explored in relation to your dinner guests and football enthusiasts. You'll be re-introduced to the marvelous prefix "re" and see how this simple little construct, when it's added to a word, can screw up your entire theology.

Prepare to see death from an entirely different perspective as *Eternal Life. Yes, Forever!* takes off the gloves and slaps the enemy senseless once again.

Eternal Life. Yes, Forever!

ISBN-13: 978-0615623542 (Custom)

ISBN-10: 0615623549

Page Count: 140 pages

Trim Size: 6" x 9" (15.24 x 22.86 cm)

Color: Black & White on White paper

Related Categories Religion / Christian Life / Spiritual Growth

www.lifeyesforever.com

DID YOU LIKE THE BOOK?

It has been my hope that contained within the contents of this book there has been one item, possibly more, which has inspired you or brought clarity to the path you're now following. If this is the case, then I would like to hear from you about what you discovered. You can write me at mike@mikehillebrecht.com.

Within the spirit of grace contained within this message, there is one of several other things you can now do. Books are promoted mostly by word of mouth. So if you found this useful, tell a friend. Heck, tell all your friends. Mention it on Facebook or whatever other social medium you use. If you're so inclined, you could go onto Amazon.com, look up the book and press the like button. While you're there, write a short review, or a long one if you like, about what you felt the book meant to you. If you're really inspired, give a copy to a pastor.

If none of these things interest you, I understand. Many of us don't feel it is right to compel others to view matters such as grace on the same plane as us. After all there are better things to have a dialogue about and not risk the chance of turning people off. But isn't that the reason that the risk was originally taken by Jesus – to turn people. So what have you got to lose? It's not you, but Christ who lives in you.

Thank you and my sincere gratitude.

Mike

www.ingramcontent.com/pod-product-compliance
Lightning Source LLC
Chambersburg PA
CBHW051824040426
42447CB00006B/363